# FINDING YOUR Rainbow IN A Sky FULL OF CLOUDS

A Blueprint To Reveal Your True Brilliance

**TERESA GRAVES, LPC-S**

Copyright © [2024] by Teresa B. Graves, LPC-S

All Rights Reserved

No portion of this book may be reproduced, distributed, stored in a retrieval system, or transmitted in any form or by any means electronic, mechanical, photocopying recording, or otherwise without the written permission of the author or publisher, except as permitted by U.S. copyright law.

This publication is licensed for your personal enjoyment only. It is designed to provide accurate and authoritative information in regard to the subject matter. It is sold with the understanding that neither the author nor the publisher is engaged in rendering medical, psychological, or other professional advice and/or services. While the author and publisher have used their best efforts in preparing this book, they make no representations or warranties with respect to the accuracy or completeness of the contents of this book and specifically disclaim any implied warranties of/for merchantability or fitness for any purpose. No warranty may be created or extended by sales representatives or written sales material. The advice and strategies herein may not be suitable for your situation. You should consult a professional when appropriate. Neither the author nor the publisher shall be liable for any loss of profit or any other commercial damages, including but not limited to special, incidental, consequential, personal, or other damages.

Book Cover by @ricacabrex on Fiverr

1st edition 2024

# Contents

Acknowledgments . . . . . . . . . . . . . . . . . . . . . . . . . . . . . . . . . v
Welcome.   Finding Your Rainbow . . . . . . . . . . . . . . . . . . . . vii

Chapter 1.  Embarking on the Journey: Opening Your Heart to Possibilities . . . . . . . . . . . . . . . . . . . . . . . 1

Chapter 2.  The Cloudy Canvas: Recognizing and Addressing Life's Challenges . . . . . . . . . . . . . . . 16

Chapter 3.  The Colors Within – Discovering Your True Self . . . . . . . . . . . . . . . . . . . . . . . . . . . . . . . . 33

Chapter 4.  Crafting Your Palette: Setting Personal Goals and Dreams . . . . . . . . . . . . . . . . . . . . . . . 48

Chapter 5.  Weathering the Changes: Building Resilience in Turbulent Times . . . . . . . . . . . . . . 72

Chapter 6.  Rainbow Mindset: Shifting Perspectives for Positivity . . . . . . . . . . . . . . . . . . . . . . . . . . . 96

Chapter 7.  Painting Your Path: Setting Goals and Creating a Vision . . . . . . . . . . . . . . . . . . . . . . . 115

Chapter 8.  Dancing in the Rain - Finding Joy in Adversity . . . . . . . . . . . . . . . . . . . . . . . . . . . . . . . 135

Chapter 9.  Connecting with Others: Building Supportive Relationships . . . . . . . . . . . . . . . . . . 152

Chapter 10. Living Your Spectrum: Creating a
            Fulfillment and Meaningful Life ........... 175
Chapter 11. A Call to Action: Empowering Change
            Through Purposeful Engagement........... 196
Conclusion. Embracing Your Rainbow Journey .......... 205

Reference ........................................... 217
About the Author.................................... 221

# Acknowledgments

My heartfelt gratitude goes to all those who supported me throughout the journey of creating and writing this book. To my loving husband, whose unwavering encouragement fueled my determination, and my family for pushing me out of my comfort zone to make my dreams a reality. I am profoundly grateful to all those who gave me the direction I needed when my resolve was not as strong. A special acknowledgment is reserved for all those who helped me throughout the incredible process of completing this work.

I extend my gratitude to you for taking the risk of stepping out of your comfort zone by reading this book. I am grateful for your willingness to explore the idea that there is a rainbow on the other side of the clouds and adopt a positive mindset, gain personal fulfillment, engage in activities that bring you joy, and surround yourself with those who uplift, support, and encourage you. Thank you.

# WELCOME

## "Finding Your Rainbow"

It is often said, "Life is a journey." This notion could be the most simple yet complicated statement ever. Life is a woven tapestry with moments of joy, sorrow, triumph, and defeat. It is a journey towards personal fulfillment, a pursuit that often requires navigating through a sky full of clouds. As we strive to make our dreams and aspirations a reality, there is no doubt we will face challenges that can cast shadows over our path. Much like dark clouds, these trials can come in various forms – obstacles, setbacks, and moments of uncertainty.

The importance of this journey lies not just in reaching the destination but in the growth and self-discovery that occur along the way. In these moments of challenge and adversity, the true essence of our character is revealed. Navigating life's challenges, including resilience, becomes a skill and a transformative process, molding us into individuals capable of weathering storms and emerging stronger on the other side.

As we embark on the quest for personal fulfillment, we must recognize that the path we take is not always lined with sunshine. The clouds we encounter are part of the human experience, each carrying valuable lessons and opportunities for growth and development. This book is a mere guide that aims to provide insights, strategies, and a roadmap for weathering life's storms and finding the beauty within them.

Throughout the following chapters, we will dive into the art of resilience, exploring the history of challenges, understanding the importance of self-awareness, and equipping ourselves with the tools needed to overcome obstacles. By the end of this journey, I hope you will discover your rainbow amidst the clouds and embrace the storms as catalysts for personal growth and fulfillment. So, let us embark on this transformative journey together, ready to face the challenges, learn from them, and emerge into the sunlight with newfound strength and perseverance.

May you find the true path to self-fulfillment and joy.

**Define the Problem** - Defining the problem entails identifying and clearly describing the issue at hand, laying the foundation for effective problem-solving and decision-making processes. It serves as a crucial step in navigating complexity, providing clarity that empowers you to strategize and implement solutions with precision and purpose.

A. **Recognition of the Clouds of Life – Obstacles, Setbacks, and Challenges:**

   Life's rich tapestry is filled with happy moments but is also peppered with difficulties that create shadows like clouds blocking the sun. These hurdles can take many forms, such as trials that require our tenacity, setbacks that test our resolve, and difficulties that try our determination. The first step toward achieving personal fulfillment is realizing these clouds and accepting that they are there. Identifying these obstacles is crucial to setting off on a path to a better future, regardless of whether our relationships, career pursuits, or personal challenges cause them.

B. **Impact of Persistent Negativity on Personal Well-being:**

   The storms of negativity that accompany clouds in our lives can undermine our well-being. These storms may be heavy and continuous. Our mental, emotional, and physical states are severely impacted when negativity takes on a dominant role in our lives. Long-term negative thinking can cause tension, worry, and a lowered sense of self-worth. Recognizing the consequences of chronic negativity is important because it can be a strong incentive to start a transformational path, build resilience, and develop an optimistic outlook that can discover the light at the end of the tunnel. In this investigation, we disentangle the complex connection between difficulties and well-being. We aim to learn how to withstand the storms and use their energy to propel our personal development forward.

## What the Reader Needs to Know Before Tackling the Problem

A. **Importance of Self-Awareness and Understanding Personal Strengths:**

Readers must understand the importance of self-awareness before they set out to locate their rainbow. Gaining self-awareness, identifying one's assets and shortcomings, and exploring one's basic principles offer a strong basis for overcoming life's obstacles. By being self-aware, you can take advantage of your special traits and use your own advantages to overcome challenges and disappointments. As you become more aware of who they are and what they can offer in the midst of difficulty, this introspective journey develops resilience.

B. **Building a Foundation of Emotional Intelligence:**

A vital component in the quest for personal fulfillment is emotional intelligence. Readers must comprehend the significance of identifying, comprehending, and regulating their own emotions as well as those of others. Possessing a high emotional intelligence gives you the ability to successfully negotiate challenging social circumstances, form deep connections, and manage the emotional toll that obstacles take. Readers get a critical skill set for navigating difficult situations and establishing a positive environment that supports well-being and personal development by cultivating emotional aptitude.

C. **Developing A Growth Mindset for Continuous Improvement:**

Having a growth mentality is a great advantage when trying to overcome obstacles. It is important for readers to know that a growth mindset is the conviction that aptitude and intelligence can be enhanced, refined, and developed with commitment and diligence. Develop a mindset that views impediments as possibilities for ongoing progress rather than insurmountable hurdles and learn to view challenges as opportunities for learning and growth. This change in perspective enables readers to see failures as learning opportunities, fostering resiliency and tenacity in the pursuit of individual objectives. Equipped with a growth mentality, you may tackle life's obstacles with hope and a dedication to continuous improvement. Gaining an understanding of these fundamental ideas paves the way for a life-changing adventure to discover your rainbow amid clouds.

**Develop an Action Plan** - Developing an action plan involves outlining specific steps, timelines, and responsibilities to achieve goals effectively and efficiently in a structured manner. Crafting an action plan is akin to drawing a roadmap to success, guiding you through a systematic approach that transforms aspirations into tangible milestones, fostering accountability and momentum along the journey.

A. **Identifying and Setting Personal Goals:**

Clearly defined and meaningful personal goals are the first steps to overcoming life's obstacles and discovering your rainbow. Spend some time thinking about your goals, values, and passions. What are the sincere goals you have for yourself regarding your well-being, relationships, work, or personal growth? A road map for your journey can be obtained by setting SMART* goals—specific, measurable, achievable, relevant, and time-bound. These objectives act as lighthouses, pointing you toward the brilliant colors of your intended results while you navigate the clouds.

B. **Creating A Roadmap for Overcoming Specific Challenges:**

Setting goals and developing a strategic plan of action are vital steps in conquering any particular obstacles that may come up. Divide your big objectives into smaller, more doable activities. Determine probable roadblocks and create backup plans. Adopt a problem-solving mentality and see obstacles as chances to improve your strategy rather than obstacles to overcome. This blueprint turns into your navigation system, guiding you through the clouds with resilience and purpose. Review and modify your itinerary frequently and be flexible to accommodate unforeseen detours on your travels.

C. **Cultivating A Positive and Resilient Mindset:**

Developing a resilient and upbeat mindset is essential to the action plan. Develop the mentality that views obstacles as chances for improvement. Show appreciation for what you have, even in the midst of challenges, pay attention to the good things in your life. Instead of viewing setbacks as failures, view them as teaching opportunities. Create a positive environment for yourself by engaging in thoughtful activities, encouraging content, and supporting connections. Recognize your skills and celebrate your accomplishments, no matter how modest, to build resilience. A resilient and upbeat attitude can help you weather the storms and see the beauty concealed beneath the clouds you encounter on your path.

In the vast landscape, challenges often manifest as clouds and shadows on your journey. These challenges, like storms, can potentially obscure your path and dampen your spirit. Cultivating a positive and resilient mindset, however, is the key to navigating this intricate terrain. Such a mindset acts as a beacon, guiding you through the darkest clouds and enabling you to perceive beauty hidden within the storms.

A positive mindset is a powerful force that transforms obstacles into opportunities for growth. When faced with adversity, those with a positive outlook tend to view challenges not as hurdles but as chances to learn, adapt, and evolve. This perspective shift allows them to weather the storms with a sense of purpose and determination, knowing that every challenge is a stepping stone toward personal development.

Resilience, on the other hand, is the sturdy vessel that carries you through turbulent times. It empowers you to persevere when the journey becomes arduous, reminding you that even in the midst of storms, there exists an opportunity to emerge stronger and wiser.

The metaphor of clouds holds a profound truth – within the turbulence lies beauty waiting to be discovered. Challenges often conceal hidden treasures like the silver lining gracing a dark cloud's edge. A positive and resilient mindset enables you to unveil these treasures, extracting valuable lessons and insights from every experience, no matter how daunting.

Moreover, a resilient mindset encourages you to find joy in the process, even amidst difficulties. It instills the belief that challenges, like storms, are temporary and that beyond them awaits clearer skies. This understanding allows you to appreciate the beauty of their journey, recognizing that the contrast of light and shadow enhances the overall tapestry of your life.

In essence, embracing a positive and resilient mindset transforms the journey through life into a profound adventure. It turns challenges into opportunities, storms into sources of strength, and clouds into canvases on which the art of resilience is painted. As you navigate the unpredictable terrain of existence, remember that the most captivating beauty often emerges from the heart of the storm, and a mindset fortified with positivity and resilience serves as the compass guiding you toward the discovery of that beauty.

By actively implementing these steps—**setting meaningful goals, creating a strategic roadmap**, and **cultivating a positive mindset**—you empower yourself to proactively navigate challenges, fostering personal growth and resilience to find your rainbow in a sky full of clouds.

**Expand Outward: Applying New Knowledge and Skills** - Expanding outward involves integrating newly acquired knowledge and skills into various aspects of your life or work, fostering continuous growth and development. It encompasses the dynamic process of assimilating newfound expertise and insights across diverse domains, catalyzing a ripple effect that propels personal and professional evolution towards greater excellence and innovation.

A. **Navigating Future Challenges with Newfound Resilience:**

Armed with the resilience cultivated through your journey, facing future challenges becomes an opportunity for growth rather than a daunting prospect. Understand that challenges are a natural part of life, and the lessons have fortified your ability to navigate them. Embrace uncertainty with a newfound confidence, knowing you possess the resilience to adapt and overcome. Use past successes as a foundation for future challenges, continually refining your resilience toolkit as you encounter new clouds.

B. **Strategies for Maintaining a Positive Mindset During Times of Adversity:**

Sustaining a positive mindset is an ongoing practice, especially during the inevitable difficult times that life presents. Implement mindfulness, positive affirmations, and gratitude exercises to anchor yourself in positivity. Learn to reframe negative thoughts, finding silver linings even in the darkest clouds. Embrace self-compassion, allowing yourself the grace to navigate challenges without self-judgment. By maintaining a positive mindset during difficult times, you not only endure the storms but also emerge with a greater appreciation for the strength within.

C. **Dealing With Others Stuck in Old Patterns:**

*As* you evolve, you may encounter others entrenched in old patterns or struggling with their own clouds. Develop empathy and effective communication skills to navigate these interactions. Seek to understand their perspectives without judgment, recognizing that everyone is on their unique journey. Communicate with kindness and clarity, offering support and encouragement. Lead by example, demonstrating the positive transformation that can result from embracing change. You contribute to a more supportive and understanding community by fostering empathy and effective communication.

D. **Establishing a Support Network and Seeking Help When Needed:**

*No* journey is meant to be traveled alone. Establish a strong support network of friends, family, mentors, and like-minded people who understand and encourage your growth. Surround yourself with people who uplift and inspire you. When facing particularly challenging clouds, don't hesitate to seek professional help or guidance. Therapy, coaching, or mentorship can provide valuable insights and strategies for navigating complex situations. Recognize the strength in vulnerability, understanding that asking for help is a courageous act that contributes to your overall resilience.

Embarking on a journey of personal and communal growth involves expanding your horizons and applying newfound knowledge and skills to navigate the challenges ahead. The critical components of this transformative journey include resilience, a positive mindset, empathy and communication, and the establishment of a robust support network. These elements shape your path and contribute significantly to creating a more resilient and compassionate community.

Resilience becomes a cornerstone in facing adversities, allowing you to bounce back from setbacks and grow stronger in the face of challenges. By cultivating resilience, you adapt to change, turn obstacles into opportunities, and maintain a forward momentum in your personal development. This resilience is beneficial on an individual level and ripples outward, influencing the broader community to face collective challenges with determination and strength.

Maintaining a positive mindset further amplifies the transformative power of personal growth. Positivity fosters a mindset that seeks solutions rather than dwelling on problems, enabling you to approach challenges with optimism and creativity. This outlook not only propels personal development but also contributes to the overall atmosphere of a community. A positive community is more likely to collaborate, innovate, and support one another, fostering an environment conducive to growth and well-being.

Practicing empathy and effective communication solidifies the connections between individuals, creating a web of understanding and shared experiences. Empathy bridges gaps, fosters inclusivity, and promotes a sense of unity within a community. Effective communication, on the other hand, ensures that ideas, concerns, and solutions are conveyed transparently, fostering a culture of collaboration and mutual support. Empathy and communication lay the foundation for a community that values diverse perspectives and works cohesively toward common goals.

Finally, the establishment of a robust support network cements the idea that personal growth is not a solitary endeavor. A community built on strong interpersonal connections provides a safety net for individuals, offering encouragement, guidance, and shared experiences. This interconnectedness transforms challenges from isolated struggles into communal opportunities for growth and resilience.

In short, by expanding outward and integrating resilience, a positive mindset, empathy and communication, and a robust support network into their personal journeys, you contribute significantly to the creation of a more resilient and compassionate community. This holistic approach to growth transforms you and fosters an environment where the collective strength of a community becomes a powerful force for positive change.

By expanding outward and applying your new knowledge and skills in these areas—**navigating future challenges with resilience, maintaining a positive mindset, practicing empathy and communication,** and **establishing a robust support network**—you enhance your personal journey and contribute to a more resilient and compassionate community. Your growth becomes a beacon, inspiring others to find their own rainbow amidst the clouds.

# CHAPTER 1

## "Embarking on the Journey: Opening Your Heart to Possibilities"

### Embracing the Storm - Understanding Life's Challenges

Life, like nature, is characterized by an ever-changing landscape. It is a journey filled with peaks of joy and valleys of adversity. This opening chapter delves into the essence of life's challenges, exploring metaphorical storms that often cloud our path. It is not avoiding the storm but learning to navigate through it, discovering the transformative power that lies within.

## The Nature of Life's Challenges

The difficulties you face are the threads that crisscross the complex fabric of your life. Challenges can take many shapes, from the seemingly insignificant to the extremely important or urgent. They might be impediments, setbacks, or uncertain periods. They can be as fleeting as a passing shower or as enduring as a relentless storm, each carrying the potential to shape your character and redefine your journey.

Understanding life's challenges begins with acknowledging their inevitability. No one is immune to difficulties; they are an inherent part of the human experience. However, these can try your resilience and adaptability when you are forced to confront them. Frequently, you encounter unforeseen circumstances that test your flexibility and tenacity. These storms may manifest in personal relationships, career pursuits, health struggles, or existential questions. It is critical to understand that these difficulties are not discrete issues, but threads woven across the larger story of your life.

Creating a complex fabric that defines your existence's essence involves following a path of self-awareness. Challenges, varied in their forms and magnitudes, crisscross your life's journey, leaving an indelible mark on your character and shaping the direction of your path. These issues manifest in diverse ways, from transient impediments to enduring tempests, and vary in scale from apparently trivial to the significantly consequential.

The recognition and understanding of life's challenges commence with acknowledging that no one traverses the human experience unscathed by difficulties. Each challenge becomes a test, assessing the depth of your resilience and adaptability when confronted with life's unpredictable twists. Whether akin to passing showers or relentless storms, these challenges are potent forces capable of transforming your character and reshaping the narrative of your life.

Importantly, life's difficulties are not isolated incidents, but interconnected threads woven into the larger tapestry of your existence. They show up in a variety of contexts, such as the complexities of intimate relationships, achieving career objectives, dealing with health issues, and existential contemplation. To comprehend these difficulties, you must acknowledge them as essential elements of your life narrative, each adding to the overall depth of your experiences.

In navigating the unpredictable terrain of life, embracing the ebb and flow of challenges is crucial, for they are not roadblocks but rather pathways to growth. By acknowledging their inevitability, you cultivate a mindset that allows you to confront difficulties with resilience and adaptability, understanding that each challenge is a thread contributing to the intricate and evolving fabric of your life.

## ■ The Transformative Power of Adversity

Adversity, rather than being an enemy, holds the key to transformation. It is within the storm that you develop the strength to overcome it. Adversity pushes you beyond your comfort zones, urging you to tap into the reservoirs of resilience deep within you that you may not have otherwise known existed. Difficulties sharpen your character like a chisel, bringing out the best in you and exposing your genuine self.

Consider a forest of trees standing against the winds. The strongest trees are not those sheltered from the storms but are those that have weathered countless disturbances, their roots reaching deep into the soil for stability. Similarly, life's challenges are the winds that sculpt your character, shaping you into an individual capable of withstanding the fiercest storms.

In its myriad forms, adversity has the potential to thrust you beyond the boundaries of your comfort zones. It disrupts the status quo, challenging you to navigate the storm and emerge stronger emotionally and mentally thus more resilient on the other side. Like a vessel, adversity refines your character, separating the impurities from the core of your being. In the pot of challenges, you can discover the reservoirs of resilience that may have remained dormant had you not been tested.

Often, during the most challenging times, you can tap into an innate wellspring of strength, courage, and determination.

Adversity is the mirror that reflects your true self, revealing facets of your character that may have gone unnoticed in the absence of turmoil. Just as pressure transforms coal into diamonds, difficulties can bring out the best in you, refining your essence and illuminating the depth of your capabilities.

The storms of life, with their unpredictable turbulence, serve as catalysts for growth. They can compel you to evolve, adapt, and overcome. Your struggles become the chisel that shapes your character, carving out resilience, empathy, and wisdom. Each trial becomes a unique stroke in the canvas of your life, contributing to the intricate design of your character.

Adversity is not the enemy but the ally on the journey of self-discovery and transformation. Within the storms of life, you can find the strength to overcome, the resilience to endure, and the character to thrive. Embracing adversity as a catalyst for growth allows you to navigate the intricate life's landscapes with grace, emerging from each challenge with a deeper understanding of yourself and the world around you.

## The Role of Perception in Facing Challenges

Embracing the storm requires a shift in perception. Challenges are not roadblocks that can never be breached but are opportunities for growth and exploration. How we perceive and interpret the events in our lives profoundly influences our ability to navigate them. Adopting a mindset that views impediments as stepping stones rather than stumbling blocks lays the foundation for resilience.

Consider reframing challenges and struggles as mediums for change. When faced with an obstacle, ask yourself: What can I learn? How can I grow through this experience? Instead of seeing obstacles as barriers that hinder progress, consider them as invitations to embark on a journey of self-discovery and empowerment. This introspective questioning becomes a compass, guiding you toward extracting meaning and lessons from adversity. This shift in perception transforms challenges into opportunities for self-discovery and empowerment.

The lens through which you perceive and interpret the events in your life holds the power to shape your resilience and capacity to navigate tumultuous times. To embrace the storm is to reframe challenges and struggles as catalysts for change.

In this mindset shift, challenges cease to be mere hindrances; they become transformative agents. Each obstacle is an opportunity to delve deeper into your capabilities, unearth hidden strengths, and develop a mindset that thrives in the face of adversity. By embracing challenges, you weather the storm and harness its energy to propel you further toward your ultimate goal.

## The Beauty Within the Clouds

Amidst life's storms, a hidden beauty exists giving you an opportunity to discover your inner strength, resilience, and capacity for growth. Just as rainbows emerge after a rain, your most profound self-realization moments often follow your life's' darkest periods. During these, you can unearth qualities within yourself that may have remained dormant in the absence of adversity.

In understanding life's challenges, it becomes clear that the clouds cast shadows and create the backdrop against which your strengths and capabilities shine the brightest. Rather than darkening your path, the storms illuminate it, highlighting your potential's rich colors.

In the intricate dance of life amidst its storms lies a hidden beauty that reveals itself in the form of your inner strength, resilience, and capacity for growth. Much like the emergence of a vibrant rainbow after a heavy downpour, your most profound opportunities for self-realization often follow your life's darkest periods. Within these challenging moments, you have the opportunity to explore the depths of your character, unveiling qualities and strengths that might have otherwise remained hidden in the absence of adversity.

Life's storms, with their tumultuous winds and relentless rains, mirror your challenges and difficulties. However, rather than viewing these challenges as obstacles solely meant to darken your path, it is crucial to recognize them as essential elements in the canvas of your existence. The clouds cast shadows that, in turn, create a backdrop against which your strengths and capabilities can shine the brightest. The storms, far from being harbingers of doom, serve as illuminating forces, revealing the richness of your abilities in vibrant hues.

In the face of adversity, you must dig deep within yourself to discover untapped reservoirs of resilience and strength. During these challenging times, you often realize the true extent of your capabilities. Like a vessel, life's storms can refine you, shaping your character and molding you into an individual with the fortitude to weather even the fiercest storms. The challenges you confront helps you grow, propelling you to ascend to new heights and explore uncharted territories within yourself.

Moreover, in times of adversity, you can cultivate a profound sense of gratitude for the moments of peace and tranquility that follow. Just as the contrast between the stormy sky and the ensuing calm intensifies the beauty of a rainbow, the juxtaposition of life's challenges and moments of respite enhances your appreciation for the ebb and flow of existence. The contrast between the shadows cast by the storms and the brilliance that follows accentuates the mosaic of your life, creating a rich and dynamic narrative.

Rather than being viewed with trepidation, the storms of life can be embraced as teachers, guiding you toward self-discovery and personal growth. Each challenge becomes a chapter in your life's story, contributing to your character's evolution and the unfolding of your unique journey. Through the storms, you not only discover your resilience but also learn to dance in the rain, finding joy and beauty in the very midst of adversity.

Amidst life's storms, a hidden beauty exists—one that allows you to discover your inner strength, resilience, and capacity for growth. These challenges are the backdrop against which your strengths shine brightly, much like the clouds that cast shadows. Just as rainbows follow the rain, your moments of profound self-realization often emerge after life's darkest periods, illuminating the path to a deeper understanding of yourself and the world around you. Embracing the storms becomes a transformative journey, where adversity becomes the vehicle for the emergence of your most vibrant and resilient self.

Let's look at some strategies for facing these challenges:

**Strategies for Embracing the Storm** - Strategies for embracing the storm involve adopting resilient approaches to navigate challenges, fostering adaptability, and maintaining a positive mindset during turbulent times.

1. **Mindful Awareness:** Start by cultivating a conscious awareness of your challenges. Be present in the moment, acknowledging your emotions and

thoughts without judgment. Remember – there is no right or wrong, good or bad – just let your mind be in the moment. Mindfulness provides the foundation for understanding the nature of the storm and the resources you possess to navigate through it.

2. **Resilience Building:** Take action to build resilience by reframing adversity as an opportunity for growth. The storm provides you with the information you need to change paths. Develop a mindset that views challenges as a natural part of the journey, providing a necessary guide for personal development.

3. **Acceptance and Adaptation:** Embrace the art of acceptance. Some storms cannot be avoided, but your response to them can be controlled. Try as you might, you cannot control the reactions of others. Learn to adapt to changing circumstances, recognizing that flexibility is crucial to navigating rough skies.

4. **Seeking Support:** Understand that navigating storms doesn't have to be a solitary endeavor. Asking for help and support is not a statement of poor character but a declaration of true strength. Contact your support network – friends, family, mentors, or seek professional guidance. Sharing your challenges lightens the burden and invites diverse perspectives and solutions.

The concepts of mindful awareness, resilience building, acceptance and adaptation, and seeking support form a comprehensive framework for navigating life's challenges with grace and effectiveness. Mindful awareness involves cultivating a heightened consciousness of the present moment, allowing you to better understand your thoughts, emotions, and reactions. This awareness serves as the foundation for resilience building as individuals learn to respond to adversity with a balanced and composed mindset.

Resilience building, in turn, empowers you to bounce back from setbacks, view obstacles as opportunities for growth, and persist in the face of adversity. The transformative force enables you to not only withstand challenges but also emerge stronger and more capable of navigating them.

Acceptance and adaptation play crucial roles in this framework, emphasizing the importance of acknowledging and embracing the realities of life. Acceptance does not imply resignation but rather a willingness to confront and understand circumstances, fostering a mindset that is open to adaptation. Adaptation involves flexibly adjusting your strategies and perspectives to align with the ever-changing nature of life, ensuring a more harmonious and sustainable approach to your challenges.

Seeking support completes the framework by recognizing the strength derived from interpersonal connections. It involves reaching out for guidance, encouragement, and shared experiences, fostering a sense of community. This pillar reinforces the idea that strength is not found in isolation but rather in the collective support of those who understand and emphasize.

Mindful awareness, resilience building, acceptance and adaptation, and seeking support create a holistic approach to navigating life's complexities. This framework equips you with the tools needed to face challenges with resilience, adaptability, and a sense of interconnectedness, ultimately fostering personal growth and creating a supportive and empathetic community.

### Personal Reflection: A Storm Diary

To deepen your understanding of life's challenges, consider maintaining a "Storm Diary." In this journal, document the challenges you face, your emotional responses, and the strategies you employ to navigate through them. Reflect on how each storm contributes to your personal growth and resilience. Over time, this diary becomes a testament to your evolving relationship with adversity and how, with each entry, your growth will become self-evident.

Accepting the storm and understanding life's challenges pave the way for self-discovery, resilience, and transformation. The storms are not to be feared but embraced, for it is within their midst that the colors of your true self emerge. As you navigate the storms, you move closer to finding your rainbow in a sky full of clouds.

A Storm Diary is a powerful tool for personal reflection and growth, providing a structured way to navigate life's challenges and gain deeper insights into your emotional responses and coping mechanisms.

**Here are the essential elements to include in a Storm Diary:**

1. **Date and Time:**

    Begin each entry by recording the date and time of the event or challenge. This establishes a chronological record, enabling you to track patterns and progress.

2. **Description of the Challenge:**

    Clearly articulate the specific challenge or difficulty you are facing. Be clear and detailed in your description, providing context for better understanding.

3. **Emotional Responses:**

    Reflect on your emotional reactions to the challenge. Identify and express the emotions you experienced, such as fear, frustration, sadness, or even moments of resilience and strength.

4. **Strategies Employed:**

   Document the strategies and coping mechanisms you employed to navigate through the storm. This could include practical actions, emotional regulation techniques, or seeking support from others.

5. **Outcomes and Learnings:**

   Evaluate the outcomes of your efforts. Did your strategies help you overcome the challenge, or did you face setbacks? Reflect on the lessons learned and the insights gained from the experience.

6. **Personal Growth and Resilience:**

   Consider how the challenge contributed to your personal growth and resilience. Reflect on the strengths and qualities you discovered within yourself and identify any areas for improvement.

7. **Future Considerations:**

   Contemplate how you might approach similar challenges in the future. What insights can you carry forward to enhance your resilience? Consider setting intentions or goals for personal development based on your reflections.

8. **Gratitude and Positivity:**

   Conclude each entry by identifying elements of gratitude or positivity, no matter how small.

This helps to cultivate a mindset of resilience and optimism, even in the face of challenges.

9. **Additional Notes or Observations:**

    Leave space for additional notes or observations that may not fit into the specific categories but are relevant to your overall experience and reflection.

10. **Visual Elements (Optional):**

    Consider incorporating visual elements such as sketches, symbols, or colors to represent your emotions or to add a creative dimension to your reflections.

As you consistently maintain your Storm Diary, you will create a comprehensive record of your evolving relationship with adversity. Over time, you can review past entries to witness your growth, recognize patterns, and celebrate the resilience that emerges from navigating life's storms. The Storm Diary is a testament to your journey, showcasing the colors of your true self that appear amidst the clouds of challenges.

# CHAPTER 2

## "The Cloudy Canvas: Recognizing and Addressing Life's Challenges"

### Clearing the Sky: Identifying and Overcoming Obstacles

In the journey towards personal fulfillment, the landscape is often dotted with obstacles that cast shadows on our path. These impediments, whether internal or external, have the power to divert us from our goals. In this chapter, we'll explore the process of identifying and overcoming obstacles, transforming them from barriers into vehicles on the road to personal growth.

## The Nature of Obstacles

Obstacles are the challenges that push your resolve and determination to their limits. Identifying these issues is crucial in navigating the path toward personal fulfillment. Like clouds in the sky, they can obscure your vision and cast shadows on your journey, making it essential to bring them into focus.

Obstacles are formidable challenges, serving as litmus tests for your resolve and determination on the journey toward personal fulfillment. These hurdles can take various forms, manifesting in mental, emotional, physical, or external circumstances that impede progress and cast shadows on your path. In the intricate tapestry of life, identifying and understanding these roadblocks is paramount for navigating toward your goals.

Like hazes in the sky, obstacles can be as fleeting as a passing cloud or as enduring as a storm, creating moments of uncertainty and adversity. In these challenging times, your resilience and determination are tried, demanding that you confront and overcome the impediments between you and your aspirations.

Recognizing obstacles is not an admission of weakness but a courageous acknowledgment of the complexities of pursuing personal fulfillment. By bringing these challenges into focus, you can gain clarity on the hurdles that lie ahead, enabling you to develop strategies for overcoming them. Each obstacle you encounter becomes an opportunity for growth and self-discovery, a chance to strengthen your resolve and refine your determination.

Moreover, understanding obstacles requires a holistic perspective, acknowledging that challenges can emerge from various facets of life. Mental and emotional barriers may manifest as self-doubt or fear, while physical obstacles could be health-related or involve external circumstances beyond your control. Embracing the diversity of these challenges allows you to approach them with a comprehensive mindset, fostering adaptability and resilience in the face of adversity.

Obstacles are integral to personal fulfillment, trying your resolve and determination. These challenges can cast shadows on your path like clouds in the sky. However, by bringing them into focus, you can navigate through the shadows and harness the lessons in overcoming them. Embracing these challenges as opportunities for growth, you pave the way for a fulfilling journey that shapes your character and strengthens your determination to reach the summit of your aspirations.

> **Obstacles can come in two distinct categories:**

**Internal Obstacles: Self-Reflection and Awareness -** Internal obstacles involve self-reflection and awareness. Identifying and understanding personal challenges are essential steps in overcoming internal barriers to growth and fulfillment.

1. **Limiting Beliefs:** One of the most significant internal obstacles stems from limiting beliefs – deep-seated convictions about yourself and your abilities. Often formed in response to past experiences, these beliefs can act as barriers you impose on yourself. Understanding and challenging these beliefs is a crucial aspect of overcoming internal obstacles.

   Limiting beliefs are like invisible chains, formed from past experiences and self-perceptions. Recognizing and challenging these convictions is pivotal for personal growth. By dismantling these internal barriers, you can unlock your true potential, fostering resilience, and paving the way for transformative change.

2. **Fear of Failure:** This fear can incapacitate progress, preventing you from taking necessary risks and stepping outside your comfort zone. Understanding the roots of this fear and reframing failure as a natural part of the learning process allows you to overcome this internal obstacle.

   The fear of failure often stalls growth, trapping you within your comfort zones. By delving into the roots of this fear and reframing failure as a crucial facet of learning, you can liberate yourself from its paralyzing grip. Embracing failure becomes a mechanism for resilience, innovation, and personal evolution.

3. **Lack of Self-Confidence:** Poor self-confidence can impede your ability to pursue goals and aspirations. Identifying areas where confidence may be lacking and actively working towards building self-assurance is a transformative step in overcoming internal obstacles.

   Lack of self-confidence acts as a silent barrier, hindering goal pursuit. Identifying areas of self-doubt and proactively cultivating confidence is pivotal for personal growth. This transformative journey involves embracing challenges, celebrating successes, and gradually building the self-assurance needed to pursue aspirations with resilience and conviction.

**External Obstacles: Navigating the External Landscape -** External obstacles require navigating the external landscape. Understanding and adapting to external challenges foster resilience and empowers you to overcome impediments in your journey.

1. **Environmental Challenges:** External factors, such as economic conditions, societal expectations, or geographical limitations, can pose significant obstacles. Recognizing and assessing these external

challenges allows for strategic planning and adaptation to overcome or navigate around them.

Environmental challenges, rooted in external factors, demand strategic awareness and adaptability. By recognizing economic conditions, societal expectations, or geographical limitations, you can craft informed plans. This proactive approach enables you to navigate or surmount external obstacles, fostering resilience and a dynamic response to the ever-changing external landscape.

2. **Relationship Dynamics:** While enriching your life, relationships can also present as obstacles. Conflicts, unsupportive environments, or toxic relationships can hinder your personal growth. Identifying and addressing these dynamics is vital in creating a conducive space and overcoming obstacles.

    Navigating relationships involves acknowledging that conflicts or toxicity are unproductive and prevent you from moving forward in your pursuit of personal growth. Identifying and addressing these dynamics is pivotal for fostering a supportive environment. By cultivating healthy relationships and addressing challenges constructively, you create a conducive space for personal development, overcoming obstacles, and achieving a harmonious balance in your life.

**Time Management and Commitment:** A common external obstacle is managing time effectively, especially in the face of numerous commitments. This can be very challenging. Developing time management skills and setting priorities are instrumental in navigating external obstacles related to conflicting responsibilities.

Time management and commitment are external challenges that demand strategic navigation. Balancing numerous commitments requires honing time management skills and setting clear priorities. By effectively allocating time and staying committed to essential tasks, you can streamline your efforts, fostering resilience and successfully overcoming external obstacles tied to competing priorities.

The concept of internal obstacles, encompassing self-reflection and awareness, and external obstacles involving navigating the external landscape provide a dual perspective for addressing challenges in life. Internal obstacles require a profound journey of self-discovery and introspection. By fostering self-reflection and awareness, you can identify limiting beliefs, biases, and patterns that may hinder your personal growth. This internal exploration allows for a deeper understanding of yourself and provides the groundwork for overcoming internal barriers.

On the other hand, external obstacles involve navigating the complexities of the world around you. This requires a keen awareness of the external landscape, including societal, economic, and environmental factors. Navigating external obstacles involves developing adaptability, strategic thinking, and problem-solving skills. It requires you to proactively understand and respond to the dynamic forces shaping your external environment.

Together, addressing both internal and external obstacles creates a well-rounded approach to overcoming challenges. Internal self-reflection and awareness provide the inner strength and clarity needed to navigate the external landscape effectively. By integrating these two aspects, you can cultivate resilience, adaptability, and a holistic understanding of the factors influencing your personal journey, fostering a more comprehensive and effective approach to overcoming life's obstacles.

Let's look at some strategies for tackling these challenges:

### Strategies for Overcoming Obstacles

Overcoming obstacles requires a multifaceted approach that encompasses both internal and external strategies. Here are some ideas for effective strategies for navigating challenges:

1. **Mindful Assessment:** Begin by carefully assessing your internal and external landscape. Reflect on

your obstacles and categorize them into internal and external factors. This awareness forms the foundation for targeted efforts to overcome these challenges.

Mindful assessment is the cornerstone of overcoming obstacles. Deliberately scrutinizing internal and external factors fosters a clear understanding of challenges. Categorizing them sets the stage for targeted efforts, enabling you to navigate your journey with intentionality and strategic focus, laying the groundwork for effective and purposeful problem-solving.

2. **Goal Realignment:** Revisit your goals in light of the identified obstacles. Consider whether any adjustments or realignment of objectives is necessary. This flexible approach ensures your goals remain attainable despite the hurdles that may arise.

   Goal realignment is a dynamic response to recognized barriers. Revisiting objectives with flexibility allows for adjustments, ensuring goals remain achievable amidst challenges. This adaptive approach promotes resilience, enabling you to navigate setbacks with strategic adjustments, maintaining progress toward your aspirations.

3. **Developing A Resilient Mindset:** Cultivate a resilient mindset that views obstacles not as insurmountable barriers but as opportunities.

Embrace setbacks as learning experiences and reframing challenges as steps toward your personal development.

Developing a resilient mindset transforms obstacles into mechanisms for growth. Once you embrace setbacks as invaluable lessons, then challenges become stepping stones for personal development. This mindset shift empowers you to navigate difficulties with optimism, fortitude, and a proactive approach, ensuring your continuous growth and progress.

4. **Seeking Guidance and Support:** Don't hesitate to seek guidance from mentors, peers, or professionals. External perspectives can provide valuable insights and strategies for overcoming obstacles. A support network also offers encouragement during challenging times.

    Seeking guidance and support is a strength, not a weakness. Outside viewpoints from mentors, peers, or professionals offer valuable insights and strategies, enhancing problem-solving capabilities. Building a robust support network not only provides practical advice but also serves as a source of encouragement, fostering resilience and a sense of collective strength.

5. **Skill Development:** Identifying specific skills you can attain or already possess can help you navigate and overcome obstacles. Whether it's improving

communication skills, enhancing problem-solving abilities, or building emotional intelligence, skill development empowers you to face challenges with confidence.

Skill development is a strategic tool for overcoming obstacles. Identifying and honing specific skills equips you with the confidence to navigate challenges effectively. This ongoing process empowers continuous growth, fostering adaptability and resilience in the face of diverse adversity.

By combining these internal and external strategies, you can build a comprehensive toolkit for overcoming obstacles. This integrated approach fosters resilience, adaptability, and a proactive mindset, enabling you to navigate life's challenges more successfully. In short, by harmonizing internal strength with strategic external responses, you empower yourself to confront and overcome life's challenges effectively and with enduring fortitude.

## Personal Narrative: Conquering the Mountains

Consider viewing your journey as an ascent up a mountain. Each obstacle you encounter, then is a peak to conquer. As you climb, you gain new perspectives, strength, and resilience. The clouds begin to clear with each summit, revealing a broader landscape of possibilities.

This metaphorical climb represents a physical journey and a profound inner odyssey. As you ascend, obstacles are challenges waiting to be conquered, each peak a testament to your growth, strength, and resilience. Documenting this journey through a personal narrative allows you to celebrate each triumph and gain insights into the evolving landscape of possibilities.

**Here are some essential elements to include in your personal narrative:**

1. **Introduction - Setting the Stage:**

    Begin your personal narrative by introducing the metaphorical mountain and the journey ahead. Set the stage by describing your initial challenges and aspirations that drive you.

2. **The Peaks - Obstacles to Conquer:**

    Identify and describe each obstacle as a peak to conquer. Outline the specific challenges, whether they are related to personal growth, relationships, career pursuits, or other aspects of life. Articulate the emotions and uncertainties associated with each obstacle.

3. **The Climbing Experience - Personal Growth and Resilience:**

    Detail your experiences and emotions as you climb each peak. Highlight the moments of struggle, self-discovery, and growth. Describe how overcoming these obstacles contributed to your personal development, building resilience and grit.

4. **New Perspectives - Insights and Learnings:**

    With each conquered peak, gain new perspectives. Reflect on the insights and learnings acquired during the ascent. How has overcoming challenges broadened your understanding of yourself and the world around you? What valuable lessons have you gathered?

5. **The Clearing Skies - Reaping the Rewards:**

    Emphasize the positive transformations as the clouds begin to clear with each summit. Illustrate how conquering obstacles opens up a broader landscape of possibilities and reveals the rewards of your perseverance.

6. **Documenting Triumphs - Celebrate Your Progress:**

    Celebrate each conquered obstacle as a triumph. Document your achievements, no matter how small, and express gratitude for the lessons learned. This creates a positive narrative that reinforces your determination and resilience.

7. **Reflection and Integration - Integrating Experiences:**

   Take moments for reflection between peaks. How have the challenges and triumphs shaped your character? How do they contribute to the overall narrative of your life's journey? Integrate these experiences into your evolving understanding of self.

8. **The Summit - Ultimate Aspirations:**

   Describe the ultimate summit of your journey—the culmination of your aspirations. What does success and fulfillment look like for you? Share your vision for the future, acknowledging that the journey is ongoing.

By documenting your journey as an ascent up a mountain, you create a personal narrative that captures the essence of your growth, resilience, and triumphs. This narrative becomes a powerful tool for self-reflection, providing a roadmap for your ongoing ascent and a source of inspiration for future challenges.

## The Transformative Power of Overcoming Obstacles

Overcoming obstacles is not about removing barriers; it is a transformative process that shapes character and builds resilience. The very act of facing and conquering challenges instills a sense of empowerment and self-efficacy. It reshapes the narrative of your journey, transforming obstacles into personal growth milestones.

By identifying and overcoming obstacles, you clear the sky of limitations, allowing the brilliance of your potential to shine through. The journey becomes about reaching the destination and evolving into a person capable of navigating any terrain with grace and resilience. Once perceived as impediments, obstacles become integral elements of the landscape – a testament to your strength and determination.

Overcoming obstacles is not merely removing barriers but a profound and transformative process that forges character and fortifies resilience. It is a dynamic journey where challenges serve as sculptors, shaping the contours of our identity and instilling a profound sense of empowerment and self-efficacy within you. Facing and conquering these challenges becomes a rite of passage, a testament to your inner strength and the capacity to thrive amidst adversity.

In the ordeal of overcoming obstacles, a metamorphosis occurs. It goes beyond the external triumphs and delves into the internal landscape, reshaping the narrative of your journey. Each conquered challenge becomes a milestone of personal growth, etching a story of determination, resilience, and evolving capabilities. The scars from these battles become not wounds but badges of honor, marking your progress on the transformative path you tread.

Moreover, identifying and overcoming obstacles acts as a clarifying force, dispelling the clouds of limitations that may shroud your potential. As barriers are dismantled, the brilliance of your capabilities emerges, radiating through the once-obscured sky. The journey transcends the mere pursuit of a destination; it becomes an odyssey of personal evolution, a quest to become a person capable of navigating any terrain with grace and resilience.

The shift in perception is profound. Once perceived as impediments, obstacles morph into the landscape's integral elements, contributing to your experiences' richness. They become not roadblocks but stepping stones, evidence of your capacity to transform challenges into opportunities for growth. The resilience forged in overcoming obstacles equips you to face the uncertainties of life with newfound strength, allowing you to dance with grace through the ebb and flow of challenges.

In essence, the journey of overcoming obstacles is a transformative symphony, composing the melody of resilience and self-discovery. It propels you beyond the limitations you impose on yourself, revealing the vastness of your potential. As you continue to conquer peaks and navigate valleys, the landscape of your life becomes a testament to the enduring spirit within you—an ever-evolving masterpiece shaped by the transformative power of overcoming obstacles.

## Embracing the Journey Forward

As you navigate the process of identifying and overcoming obstacles, remember each challenge is an invitation for growth. Embrace the journey forward with a sense of purpose and resilience. Although the overall challenge may remain, the solution may become evident as you conquer each obstacle. In pursuing personal fulfillment, overcoming obstacles is not just a task but a transformative expedition toward becoming the best version of yourself.

In the tapestry of personal growth, each obstacle invites profound change. As you navigate the intricate process of identifying and overcoming challenges, view them not as hindrances but as catalysts for growth. Embrace the journey forward with purpose and resilience, recognizing that the clouds may linger, but with each conquered obstacle, the sky clears to unveil a spectrum of possibilities awaiting exploration. Pursuing personal fulfillment transcends mere tasks; it is an expedition of self-discovery and evolution. Each challenge becomes a stepping stone, propelling you toward the best version of yourself, and as you persevere, the brilliance of your potential emerges, painting the canvas of your journey with vibrant hues of resilience and purpose.

# CHAPTER 3

## "The Colors Within — Discovering Your True Self"

### Colors of Reflection – Exploring Self-Discovery and Awareness

The foundation lies in understanding your true self on the journey of personal fulfillment. This chapter is a profound exploration into the depths of self-discovery – the process of peeling away the layers to reveal the authentic hues that make you unique. It is about acknowledging your values, passions, and the intricate tapestry of your identity.

It is a transformative process that transcends the superficial and delves into the core of one's being. This introspective journey is about more than mere self-awareness; it's a conscious effort to acknowledge and embrace the values, passions, and intricate tapestry of identity that shape you as a unique person.

It involves unraveling the threads of experiences, beliefs, and aspirations woven together to form the complex fabric of who you are. Each layer peeled back is a revelation, bringing you closer to your true self's raw, unfiltered essence.

Acknowledging that values become a compass, guiding actions and decisions in alignment with your authentic principles. Unveiling passions and interests provides a roadmap to joy and fulfillment, steering you toward endeavors that resonate with the core of your being. Exploring your identity goes beyond societal expectations; it's about embracing the nuances that make you a unique and valuable contributor to the world.

This chapter of self-discovery is not a linear path; it's a dynamic, ongoing process that evolves with experiences and reflections. It requires vulnerability and courage to confront both the light and shadow aspects of yourself. In embracing the true self, you cultivate a profound sense of authenticity and lay the groundwork for a journey toward personal fulfillment that is rich, meaningful, and deeply aligned with your innermost essence.

**Unveiling the Layers: The Essence of Discovery** - The essence of discovery encapsulates the profound process of peeling away societal conditioning and internal masks. This unveiling reveals the authentic self, fostering self-discovery and the vibrant hues of genuine identity.

1. **Reflection on Core Values:** The journey of self-discovery commences with a profound reflection on your core values. What principles guide your decisions, actions, and relationships? Delving into the journey of self-discovery begins with a thoughtful examination of your core values. These intrinsic principles serve as the compass for navigating your decisions, actions, and relationships. By identifying and comprehending these values, you pave the way for authenticity, ensuring that your life aligns harmoniously with your true self. Identifying and understanding these values is fundamental to aligning your life with your authentic self.

2. **Passions and Interests:** Unlocking the depths of self-discovery involves recognizing the activities that ignite a fire within you. Exploring your passions and interests is akin to adding vibrant colors to the canvas of your identity. Whether in art, science, sports, or humanitarian efforts, these passions infuse your life with brilliance, shaping a canvas uniquely yours. What activities ignite this spark? Exploring your passions and interests is a crucial step in self-discovery.

3. **Strengths and Weaknesses:** Comprehending your strengths and weaknesses unveils the dynamics of your personality, illuminating the aspects that propel you forward and those that signify growth opportunities. This self-awareness becomes a compass guiding your personal development, fostering a journey of continual growth and improvement. In short, understanding your strengths and weaknesses clarifies the facets of your personality that propel you forward and those that present growth opportunities.

4. **Navigating Personal Narratives:** Exploring the narratives woven through your life unveils the powerful influence of personal stories have on your identity. By unraveling these narratives, you gain insight into the interplay between self-perception and societal expectations. This awareness empowers you to rewrite narratives, aligning them authentically with your evolving sense of self. Examine the narratives you've crafted about yourself throughout life. How have these stories shaped your identity? Unraveling these narratives allows you to discern between self-perception and societal expectations.

**The Art of Mindful Self-Exploration** - Mindful self-exploration involves cultivating a conscious and non-judgmental awareness of one's thoughts, emotions, and experiences. Through this intentional introspection, you navigate your inner landscape, fostering self-discovery and promoting personal growth with compassion and understanding.

Here are some strategies to assist in this endeavor:

1. **Mindfulness Practices:** Integrate mindfulness practices into your daily routine to deepen your connection with your inner self. Mindfulness meditation, journaling, or simply being present in the moment fosters self-awareness, enabling you to explore the colors within. By embracing these moments of present awareness, you deepen the connection with your inner self, allowing the vibrant colors of your thoughts and emotions to unfold and enrich the canvas of your self-discovery.

2. **Solitude and Reflection:** Allocate moments of solitude for self-reflection. In the quiet spaces of contemplation, you can sift through the layers of external influences and societal expectations to uncover your authentic desires and aspirations. By dedicating moments to solitude for self-reflection is a powerful act of reclaiming your authentic self. Amidst the quietude, you sift through external layers, discerning genuine desires and aspirations. This intentional introspection becomes a compass guiding you towards a more authentic and fulfilling life.

3. **Creative Expression:** Engage in creative outlets as a means of self-expression. Whether through art, writing, music, or any other form of creativity, these mediums provide a canvas for your inner colors to manifest. Creative expression serves as a transformative avenue for self-discovery. Through these creative outlets, you not only externalize emotions but also give form to the hues within. This artistic exploration becomes a mirror reflecting the depth and richness of your inner world.

**The Masks We Wear: Stripping Away Inauthentic Layers** - The Masks We Wear explores shedding inauthentic layers we adopt in response to societal expectations. Stripping away these masks reveals your true self, fostering authenticity, and allowing you to embrace genuine connections and self-expression.

1. **Social Conditioning:** We accumulate layers shaped by societal norms and expectations throughout life. Social conditioning weaves layers onto our identity through these societal norms. Recognizing and shedding these layers of social conditioning is a liberating process, allowing your true self to emerge. This process involves questioning inherited beliefs, fostering authenticity, and paving the way for a more genuine and fulfilling existence.

2. **Comparison and Authenticity:** The habit of comparing yourself to others often obscures the authentic self. Learn to embrace your unique journey; each color that sets you apart contributes to the masterpiece of your identity. Celebrate these distinctions, fostering self-acceptance and allowing your true colors to shine brightly. Embrace your unique journey and celebrate the colors that set you apart.

3. **Fear of Judgment:** The fear of judgment can lead to the creation of masks that conceal your true self. Fear weaves masks in multiple layers, concealing who you are. Confronting this fear liberates your authenticity and by embracing vulnerability you engage in a transformative act that unveils the genuine colors within you, fostering self-acceptance and genuine connections with others. Challenging this fear and embracing vulnerability is an essential step in revealing your authentic colors.

**The Intersection of Identity and Purpose -** The intersection of identity and purpose is the profound juncture where self-discovery aligns with a sense of purpose. In this convergence, you unearth the authentic facets of your identity, intertwining them with a meaningful life's purpose, creating a harmonious and fulfilling existence.

1. **Aligning with Purpose:** Self-discovery and a sense of purpose are intertwined. As you uncover your true self, you become better equipped to align your life with a sense of purpose. By identifying activities and pursuits harmonizing with your authentic identity, you not only navigate your path with clarity but also infuse your journey with profound meaning. Take time to identify activities and pursuits that resonate with your authentic self.

2. **Embracing Evolution:** Recognize that self-discovery is an ongoing process marked by evolution. Adopting evolution acknowledges that self-discovery is a continuous journey of growth and transformation. With each experience and lesson, your understanding of your true self deepens, revealing new layers of your uniqueness. By embracing change and welcoming this ongoing development, you nurture a dynamic and authentic relationship with yourself. Welcome change and accept the unfolding layers within you.

## Personal Growth Journal: Mapping Your Colors

Create a personal growth journal to document your discoveries. Include reflections on your values, passions, and the evolving understanding of your identity. Use this journal as a compass, guiding you towards authentic living and aligning with your true self.

A personal growth journal is a powerful tool for self-discovery. This journal serves as a benchmark, guiding you through reflections on values, passions, and the evolving understanding of your identity. A personal growth journal is a transformative sanctuary, capturing the essence of your journey.

**Here are the essential elements to include in a personal growth journal:**

1. **Date and Time:**

    Begin each entry by noting the date and time. This establishes a chronological record of your growth journey, allowing you to track progress.

2. **Reflections on Values:**

    Explore and articulate your core values. Reflect on the principles that are important to you and shape your decisions and actions. Consider how these values align with your current lifestyle and if any adjustments are needed.

3. **Passions and Interests:**

    Document your desires and pursuits. Identify hobbies or leisure activities that ignite enthusiasm and bring you joy. Reflect on incorporating more of these passions into your daily life for fulfillment and happiness.

4. **Identity Exploration:**

    Delve into the evolving understanding of your identity. Consider aspects such as your beliefs, cultural background, and personal growth. Reflect on how these elements contribute to your sense of self and how they may be developing.

5. **Goal Setting and Progress Tracking:**

    Set personal growth goals and document your progress. Outline short-term and long-term objectives, and regularly assess how your actions align with these goals. Celebrate achievements and learn from setbacks.

6. **Challenges and Obstacles:**

    Acknowledge and reflect on the challenges and obstacles you encounter. Describe the emotions associated with these difficulties and explore strategies for overcoming them. Consider how these challenges contribute to your growth.

7. **Gratitude Journaling:**

    Include a section for expressing gratitude. Write down things you are grateful for daily, fostering a positive mindset and appreciation for the positive elements contributing to your well-being.

8. **Self-Reflection Prompts:**

    Incorporate self-reflection prompts to guide your introspective journey. These prompts could include questions about your strengths, areas for improvement, and moments of personal triumph.

9. **Quotes and Inspirations:**

    Include quotes, affirmations, or inspirations that resonate with you. These can serve as motivational reminders and sources of encouragement during challenging times.

10. **Mindfulness Practices:**

    Integrate mindfulness practices into your journal, such as meditation or gratitude exercises. This helps foster self-awareness and a deeper connection with your thoughts and feelings.

11. **Personal Achievements:**

    Celebrate your achievements, both big and small. Recognize moments where you demonstrated resilience, overcame challenges, or took steps toward personal growth.

12. **Vision Board or Visual Representations:**

    Consider adding a vision board or visual representations of your goals. Images can be powerful tools to reinforce your aspirations and create a visual roadmap for your growth journey.

Maintaining a personal growth journal becomes a transformative cornerstone in your journey of self-discovery and evolution. This intentional practice provides a sacred space for introspection, weaving together the threads of your experiences, thoughts, and emotions. By consistently documenting core values, passions, strengths, weaknesses, and reflections on personal narratives, you create a living chronicle of your authentic self.

Journaling is a powerful tool for self-reflection, allowing you to witness the evolving layers of your identity over time. It captures the nuances of your growth, highlighting the subtle shifts and profound transformations. This dynamic resource becomes a guide, directing you through life's twists and turns, reminding you of your aspirations, values, and the lessons learned along the way.

Moreover, the journal serves as a reservoir of wisdom, offering insights into patterns of behavior and recurring themes in your life. It becomes a source of empowerment, enabling you to make informed decisions, set intentional goals, and navigate challenges with resilience. As you regularly engage in this reflective practice, you cultivate a deeper understanding of yourself, fostering authenticity and alignment with your true self.

A personal growth journal is not merely a record-keeping tool but a living testament to your journey. It becomes a mirror reflecting the colors of your identity, a compass guiding your authentic living, and a reservoir of self-awareness that propels you towards a purposeful and fulfilling life.

By consistently maintaining a personal growth journal with these elements, you create a dynamic and personalized resource for self-discovery and transformation. You can use this introspective exercise as a compass to help you live authentically and in harmony with who you really are.

**Embracing Your Authenticity** - Embracing Your Authenticity is a transformative embrace of your true self. It involves shedding societal expectations, overcoming fears, and celebrating the unique colors that make you authentically you, fostering self-love and genuine connections.

Discovering your true self is not an endpoint but a journey of continual exploration. It's a marathon, not a sprint. Embrace the following principles to navigate this expedition:

1. **Self-Compassion:** Treat yourself with kindness and understanding the same as you would treat anyone else. Self-discovery can bring forth vulnerabilities, and practicing self-compassion is essential in fostering a nurturing environment for your true self to flourish. In other words, give yourself a break. We are often our own worst critic when it is neither warranted nor true.

Self-compassion is the gentle embrace of your own weaknesses. Treating yourself with kindness, as you would a friend, fosters a nurturing environment for authentic growth. Granting yourself the grace to acknowledge imperfections without undue self-criticism creates space for genuine self-discovery and allows your true self to flourish.

2. **Courage in Vulnerability:** Embrace your weaknesses as a source of strength. It takes courage to peel away layers and reveal your true self. Vulnerability is not a flaw but a testament to your authenticity. It unveils the essence of genuineness, revealing the unfiltered, honest aspects of your being. It is a profound testament to your courage and strength, as it requires openness and integrity in sharing your real self with the world.

    Courage in vulnerability is an empowering journey. Unveiling authenticity demands determination, as it requires openness and honesty. Embracing vulnerability not only reveals the unfiltered aspects of your being but also serves as a profound testament to your courage, fostering genuine connections and allowing your true self to radiate authentically.

3. **Empathy Towards Others:** As you set out on your path of self-discovery, show compassion to those who are traveling a similar route. Recognize the diversity of colors that exist within you and

cultivate relationships that show you sympathetic humanity. Acknowledge the variety of hues that exist within you, cultivating an empathetic comprehension of our common human existence.

Empathy towards others, as you explore your unique journey, transcends personal boundaries. Acknowledging the diversity within yourself becomes a gateway to understanding shared humanity. By embracing empathy, you actively contribute to a collective voyage towards authenticity, connection, and the rich tapestry of the human experience.

## The Spectrum of Your Authentic Self

In concluding this exploration of self-discovery, envision your authentic self as a spectrum of vibrant colors, each representing an aspect of your unique identity. By understanding your core values, passions, strengths, and weaknesses, you reveal the intricate palette of the canvas of your life.

"The Colors Within" invites you to celebrate the authenticity that sets you apart. It beckons you to embrace the journey of self-discovery as a profound and ongoing expedition toward personal fulfillment. In peeling away the layers, you uncover not just your true self but a kaleidoscope of possibilities that await expression in the world. May you navigate this vibrant landscape with curiosity, self-compassion, and a profound appreciation for the colors within you.

# CHAPTER 4

## "Crafting Your Palette: Setting Personal Goals and Dreams"

### Beyond the Clouds: A Journey to Personal Radiance

In the grand tapestry of personal fulfillment, setting personal goals is an art form akin to selecting the colors on a painter's palette. This chapter serves as a guide into the intricacies of intentional goal setting, offering a framework for crafting a vivid and purposeful life. Just as an artist carefully chooses colors to bring a canvas to existence, you must thoughtfully select and define your aspirations to manifest the masterpiece of your dreams.

Intentional goal setting is not merely about jotting down wishes; it is a deliberate and conscious act of outlining the steps that lead to realizing your vision. It's about converting dreams into tangible objectives that serve as the brushstrokes, adding depth and detail to your canvas. Each goal becomes a hue, contributing to the overall composition and creating a harmonious blend of achievements.

As we embark on this journey of intentional goal setting, you must understand the art of weaving aspirations into actionable goals. It involves breaking down overarching dreams into manageable, measurable, and time-bound objectives. These goals serve as the scaffolding upon which the structure of personal fulfillment stands.

Just as an artist envisions the final artwork before placing the first brushstroke, intentional goal setting requires a clear vision of the overarching endgame. It demands self-reflection and understanding personal values, ensuring the selected goals align with your ideals and essence. This alignment infuses passion and purpose into pursuing these goals, transforming them from mere tasks into meaningful milestones.

In this chapter, you are encouraged to view your life as a canvas waiting to be adorned with purposeful brushstrokes. The strokes, representing intentional goals, breathe life into the backdrop, creating a narrative of achievements, growth, and self-realization. Through deliberate goal setting, you not only shape your destiny but also cultivate the skills of resilience, determination, and adaptability – the very essence of a well-painted and purposeful life.

**The Power of Purposeful Goals** - The potential of purposeful goals to offer guidance and inspiration is what gives them their power. Your journey of self-discovery, progress, and fulfillment is guided with intention and purpose by meaningful goals that are clear and in line with who you really are.

1. **Clarifying Your Vision:** Start by outlining your goals for personal satisfaction. What does a rewarding life look like? Envision the kaleidoscope of a satisfying life, defining your aspirations. These essential characteristics are the first paint brushstrokes that shape the portrait of your intentional and purposeful existence. Describe the general contours of your goals, covering a range of areas including work, relationships, personal growth, and wellbeing.

    Determining the specifics of your intended life is like painting the canvas of your personal contentment. These initial actions lay the groundwork for developing a deliberate and meaningful existence.

2. **Aligning Goals with Values:** Goals that align with your core values form the basis of purposeful

living. Identify the values integral to your authentic self, ensuring that your goals are achievable and resonate with the essence of who you are. Aligning goals with your core values is the bedrock of this important journey. This alignment ensures not only the achievability of your aspirations but also resonates profoundly with the essence of who you are, fostering a life rich in meaning and authenticity.

A meaningful and peaceful life is produced when your goals are in line with your basic beliefs. This combination ensures that your objectives are profoundly consistent with who you truly are and are also realistic. Setting and achieving goals in line with your values acts as an anchor that promotes a meaningful, real, and deeply purposeful existence.

3. **Integrating Passion and Purpose:** Integrate your interests into the design of your objectives. Passion-driven goals have a significant influence on resilience and motivation. They give your path meaning and turn the goal into a fulfilling experience. When passion and purpose are combined, goals become a vibrant and dynamic tapestry. Goals become sources of deep motivation and resilience when they are interwoven with your passions, beyond just serving as benchmarks. This integration gives your path a clear purpose and transforms the goal into a meaningful and genuine way to express who you really are.

When passion and purpose are combined, achieving goals becomes a rich and rewarding experience. When your goals are infused with the vitality of your passions, they transcend beyond mere accomplishments and become significant sources of resilience and drive. This dynamic fusion gives your path a sense of authenticity, allowing each step to meaningfully express who you really are.

## The S.M.A.R.T. Approach to Goal Setting

This strategy was originally developed by George Doran, Arthur Miller, and James Cunningham in their 1981 article "There's a S.M.A.R.T Way to Write Management Goals and Objectives," and is a useful tool that can be applied here.

1. **Specific:** Clearly define your goals. Instead of vague aspirations, articulate precisely what you want to achieve. Specificity provides a roadmap of your journey, offering clarity on the destination.

2. **Measurable:** Establish measurable criteria to track progress. Quantify your goals, enabling you to gauge success and identify areas for adjustment. Measurable goals provide tangible milestones on your path.

3. **Achievable:** Make sure that your goals are realistic and attainable. While it's essential to dream big, setting achievable goals prevents the

discouragement that may arise from pursuing objectives that are beyond your current capacity.

4. **Relevant:** Align your goals with your broader vision and values. Relevance ensures that your goals contribute meaningfully to your overall sense of purpose, creating a harmonious connection between your aspirations and your authentic self.

5. **Time-Bound:** Set clear timeframes for your goals. Establishing deadlines creates a sense of urgency and structure. Time-bound goals provide a sense of direction and prevent procrastination.

**Navigating Short-Term and Long-Term Goals** - Finding a balance is necessary to manage both short- and long-term objectives. Short-term goals provide immediate direction, while long-term ones offer a broader vision. Integrating both ensures a purposeful journey, with short-term actions contributing to long-term aspirations, creating a harmonious and sustainable path of personal growth.

1. **Short-Term Goals:** Your long-term vision is reached by taking these actions. Short-term objectives that can be completed in a set amount of time gives you a feeling of momentum and advancement. These are the quick brushstrokes that add to your life's changing canvas.

## Elements for Setting Short-Term Goals:

A. **Clarity and Specificity:**

Clearly define each short-term goal with specific details. Ambiguity can lead to confusion, so objectives must be explicit and well-defined. Clarity is the compass for short-term goals. By clearly defining each objective with specific details, ambiguity dissipates, ensuring your path is focused and precise.

B. **Realistic and Achievable:**

Realistic and doable in a short amount of time are the best qualities for short-term objectives. Overly ambitious goals can be demoralizing, while realistic ones bring you a feeling of success. Achieving development requires setting realistic short-term goals within a brief timeframe which ensures a sense of accomplishment, motivating further efforts without the discouragement of an overly ambitious target.

C. **Measurable Milestones:**

Divide every short-term objective into quantifiable benchmarks. This procedure enables you to monitor your progress and gives you a sense of accomplishment when you complete each step. Progress tracking is made easier when short-term objectives are divided into measurable targets. Reaching each goal gives you a sense of achievement and inspires you to go on to the next phase.

D. **Timeline:**

Give each short-term objective a precise deadline. Having a time limit gives the process structure and a sense of urgency, whether the aim is weekly, monthly, or quarterly. A clear timetable for short-term objectives gives the goal-setting process direction and importance, encouraging accountability and targeted advancement.

E. **Relevance to Long-Term Vision:**

Make sure every one of your short-term objectives supports and advances your long-term vision. The significance of short-term goals cannot be overstated, as they serve as stepping stones towards the larger picture. Setting and achieving short-term goals requires alignment with this overarching concept. They serve as integral pillars, ensuring each contributes meaningfully to the grand picture of your overarching aspirations.

F. **Actionable Steps:**

Break every short-term goal down into doable steps. These stages need to provide a clear strategy for achieving your goals and be practical and achievable. By efficiently dividing short-term objectives into manageable chunks you create a helpful success guide. These practical and helpful steps serve as a clear roadmap that sharpens your concentration and expedites your goal fulfillment.

G. **Adaptability:**

Adaptability is a key pillar for short-term goals. For short-term objectives, flexibility is essential, and you must be ready to adjust to changing circumstances. Progress and resilience are ensured by the capacity to adapt in the face of unforeseen obstacles or possibilities.

H. **Celebration and Recognition:**

Create a method for acknowledging and applauding yourself when you have met your short-term objectives. Acknowledgment strengthens a positive outlook and inspires you to approach upcoming goals with greater enthusiasm. Rewarding yourself for achieving short-term goals starts a positive feedback loop and recognition cultivates a success mindset, igniting excitement for pursuing next objectives with renewed drive and resolve.

2. **Long-Term Goals:** Long-term goals serve as the panoramic landscape that encapsulates your overarching vision. These goals define the grand picture of your aspirations, acting as the anchor for your short-term pursuits. Long-term goals provide a sense of purpose and direction.

**Elements for Setting Long-Term Goals:**

A. **Big Picture Vision:**

Describe your main idea in clear terms. Your long-term objectives should tell the whole story of what you hope to accomplish in the far future. This represents the compass for your overarching vision. Setting out your main objectives in clear terms helps to make sure that long-term objectives flow together and tell the story of your far-off future accomplishments.

B. **Goal-Setting Tools:**

For your long-term objectives, use tried-and-true goal-setting techniques, such as S.M.A.R.T. or other such processes. This procedure guarantees that they are realistic and well-defined, offering a strong basis for their pursuit. Using these goal-setting approaches ensures that the strategy you use is clear and grounded, which lays a strong basis for pursuing meaningful and long-term objectives.

C. **Breakdown into Short-Term Objectives:**

Divide long-term ambitions into a number of shorter ones. By establishing a route through this hierarchical framework, your lofty goals become more feasible and manageable. Breaking them down into short-term objectives is the path to their achievement. Through the use of a tiered framework, the large picture becomes more doable and within reach overall.

D. **Align with Values:**

Ensure that your long-term goals align with your core values and principles. This alignment adds a more profound sense of purpose and meaning to your pursuits. Alignment with your fundamental ideals elevates long-term goals, ensuring their harmony between aspirations and values which infuses your interests with a profound intention and meaning, fostering a fulfilling and authentic journey.

E. **Regular Review and Reflection:**

Plan frequent assessments to evaluate your development and consider how well your long-term objectives match your changing vision. This guarantees that your goals stay relevant, permits modifications, and ensure your goals align with your core values. By reviewing your progress, you can make the necessary adjustments needed to maintain your long-term goals, guarantee they are current and responsive to your changing vision, which will promote continuous improvement and flexibility.

F. **Flexibility and Adaptation:**

Due to the changing nature of life, your overarching goals must be adaptable and flexible in order to remain viable and relevant. Goal pursuit can be robust and successful when goals are flexible enough to accommodate these changes. By incorporating flexibility and adaptability into your long-term goals, you improve the possibility of their achievement, and your overall well-being.

G. **Inspiration and Motivation:**

Long-term objectives are nourished by inspiration and motivation. Serving as anchors, these aspirations provide a continuous wellspring of encouragement, offering compelling reasons to persist through challenges and propel the journey forward.

H. **Strategic Planning:**

Create a strategic plan to accomplish long-term objectives. Set important deadlines, assign funds, and list the important actions you need to take to make your big idea a reality. Strategic planning is the compass for long-term goals. By creating this roadmap, you ensure the realization of your goals that are both intentional and achievable.

By incorporating these elements into setting short-term and long-term goals, you create a comprehensive and strategic framework for your journey toward personal and professional fulfillment. The synergy between the immediacy of short-term goals and the broader scope of long-term aspirations ensures a dynamic and purpose-driven goal-setting approach.

Short-term goals, with their immediate focus, become the stepping stones that propel you forward. Aligned with the broader canvas of long-term aspirations, they form a dynamic synergy, ensuring that every short-term achievement contributes to the overarching narrative of your personal growth. This strategic integration maximizes effectiveness, providing a purpose-driven maneuver that transforms your aspirations into tangible and sustainable accomplishments on your journey toward fulfillment.

## Personal Goal-Setting Exercise: The Vision Board

Vision boards have been used for centuries by people worldwide to manifest their desires and achieve their goals. They are said to date back to ancient Egypt, where these goals and desires were depicted in hieroglyphics. So, how do we use them today?

Creating a vision board is a powerful and creative way to manifest your desires and aspirations, serving as a visual representation of your vision for personal fulfillment. Crafting a vision board transcends mere visualization; it's a dynamic tool for manifestation. Through images, words, and symbols, it consolidates your ambitions into a tangible, visually compelling picture. This process not only clarifies goals but also fosters a deep connection with your passions, amplifying the commitment to achieving personal fulfillment.

**Here are some key elements to include in your Vision Board.**

1. **Images:** Select images that resonate with your goals and aspirations. These can include pictures of places you want to visit, images representing professional achievements, or visuals symbolizing

personal growth. Choose photographs that evoke positive emotions and align with the essence of your dreams.

2. **Quotes and Affirmations:** Integrate motivational quotes and statements that inspire and uplift you. Words are powerful and can shape thoughts and beliefs, and incorporating affirmations reinforces a positive mindset. Choose quotes that align with the goals you aim to achieve.

3. **Symbols and Icons:** Include symbols or icons that represent critical aspects of your vision. Whether it's a symbol of balance, a compass for direction, or an emblem of success, these visual elements add depth to your board and reinforce the meaning behind your goals.

4. **Colors:** Choose colors that evoke the emotions associated with your aspirations. Colors have psychological and emotional impacts and incorporating them strategically can enhance your vision board's overall mood and energy.

5. **Personal Photos:** Include pictures of yourself engaging in activities related to your goals. These personal photos remind you of your potential and the experiences you wish to cultivate. Seeing yourself actively pursuing your aspirations reinforces a sense of self-belief.

6. **Mind Map or Goal Clusters:** Organize your goals into clusters or use a mind map to connect related

aspirations visually. This helps create a holistic representation of your vision and demonstrates the interconnectedness of your desires.

7. **Timeline or Calendar:** Your goals need to have specific timelines to help achieve them. Consider including a visual representation of a calendar or timeline to your vision board. This can help you stay organized and focused on the timeframes associated with different aspects of your vision.

8. **Vision Statement:** Write a concise vision statement summarizing the overarching theme of your goals. This statement is the anchor for your vision board, providing a clear and focused expression of your aspirations.

9. **Creative Layout:** Arrange the elements on your vision board in a visually appealing and creative layout. Consider the flow and balance of the images, quotes, and symbols to create a harmonious representation of your dreams.

10. **Display:** Place your vision board in a prominent and visible location. Make sure it's noticeable, whether it's in your bedroom, office, or another frequently visited space. The constant exposure to your vision board reinforces your goals in your subconscious mind.

11. **Update and Evolve:** Periodically update your vision board to reflect changes in your goals or aspirations. As you achieve specific objectives,

replace them with new ones to keep the board dynamic and aligned with your evolving vision for personal fulfillment.

Your vision board transforms it into a substantial beacon of motivation. This designed visual representation serves as a daily cue, saturating your surroundings with inspiration. This immersive experience reinforces commitment, aligning your actions with aspirations, and fostering a proactive approach to achieving your goals.

After you've created your vision board, pick one item on it and then **TAKE ACTION** to make it a reality. Transforming your vision into reality requires proactive steps. By selecting one item from your vision board and taking decisive action, you turn aspirations into substantial achievements. This focused approach propels you towards your goals, infusing your journey with purpose and fulfillment. Once you have completed one task, pick another in a continuous process so that your vision board is a living breathing testament to your commitment for self-fulfillment.

**Overcoming Obstacles and Adjusting Goals** - Overcoming obstacles involves resilience and adaptability. When facing challenges, adjusting goals becomes a strategic response. This dynamic interplay allows for continuous progress, ensuring that setbacks become opportunities for growth, and goals remain aligned with evolving circumstances.

In pursuing any goal, two fundamental principles, embracing challenges and flexibility in adjustment, are guiding pillars, shaping the journey toward success and personal fulfillment.

1. **Embracing Challenges:** Understand that challenges are inherent in the pursuit of any goal. Adopt these challenges as opportunities for growth rather than insurmountable obstacles. Resilience is the brush that paints beauty in the face of adversity.

   Embracing challenges is not a passive acceptance but an active and transformative mindset. Each challenge presents an opportunity, a chance to push boundaries and discover reservoirs of resilience within yourself. In the face of adversity, resilience acts as a powerful brush, painting beauty onto the canvas of the journey. It transforms challenges into stepping stones, creating a narrative of strength, determination, and self-discovery. The willingness to embrace challenges is a testament to your commitment to personal and professional growth, fostering a mindset that turns obstacles into opportunities.

2. **Flexibility in Adjustment:** Be open to adjusting your goals as circumstances evolve. Assess your goals regularly and adapt them to align with your developing vision.

   Adjustment flexibility is equally important for negotiating the complex terrain of making your dreams a reality. Understanding that life is dynamic and constantly changing means developing the ability to adapt and being willing to modify your objectives. Frequent goal assessments enables you a sophisticated comprehension of evolving conditions, offering you insight into required modifications. Rather than an acknowledgement of failure, it's an expression of resilience and wisdom.

Objectives are flexible representations of your desires that can change as your life does. They are not fixed constructs. This adaptability helps you avoid stagnation and maintain a constant sense of purpose by ensuring that your goals stay in line with your evolving vision, a calculated strategy to accomplish long-term objectives. Set important deadlines, assign funds, and list the important actions you need to take to make your big idea a reality.

Moreover, the synergy between embracing challenges and flexibility in adjustment creates a resilient and adaptable mindset essential for long-term success. When challenges arise, the ability to adjust goals in response to new information or unforeseen obstacles becomes a strategic advantage. Resilience, the product of embracing challenges, becomes the catalyst for navigating uncertainties with grace and determination.

The journey toward personal fulfillment is a dynamic dance between confronting challenges with resilience and adjusting goals with flexibility. It's a process that requires a delicate balance, a harmonious interplay of determination, adaptability, and a steadfast commitment to growth. Embracing challenges and fostering flexibility in goal setting is not just a practical approach; it's a philosophy that transforms pursuing goals into a holistic and enriching experience. The ability to navigate challenges and adjust goals with grace ultimately shapes a narrative of triumph over adversity, painting a masterpiece of resilience and achievement on the canvas of your life.

**Fostering Accountability and Support** - Fostering accountability involves both personal responsibility and cultivating a supportive environment. By acknowledging commitments and seeking support, you create a powerful synergy that propels you toward your goals, providing encouragement and resilience throughout your journey.

Establishing a network of support through accountability partners and community engagement is a powerful strategy that can significantly enhance the journey toward achieving personal and professional goals.

1. **Accountability Partners:** Sharing your goals with trusted individuals who can serve as accountability partners is akin to building a bridge between your aspirations and concrete actions. These

partners offer a valuable external perspective, holding you responsible for the commitments you've made to yourself. Regular check-ins, discussions about progress, and sharing challenges with accountability partners create a supportive environment that reinforces your dedication to your goals. The interpersonal connection provides not only encouragement but also a sense of shared responsibility, making the pursuit of goals a collaborative effort.

2. **Community Support:** Engaging with communities that align with your goals amplifies the collective energy needed for sustained motivation and inspiration. Whether it's an online forum, a local group, or a professional network, being part of a community fosters a sense of belonging and shared purpose. The synergy within a supportive community becomes a driving force, propelling you forward even when faced with obstacles. Shared experiences, advice, and encouragement from community members create a robust support system that transcends individual efforts.

The dual approach of accountability partners and community support creates a comprehensive network of encouragement and shared experiences. While accountability partners provide personalized support and guidance, community engagement offers a broader perspective and diverse insights. Together, these elements form a robust support system that bolsters commitment to goals and enriches the journey with shared triumphs and a sense of collective achievement. In a world where interconnectedness is increasingly valued, leveraging these relationships becomes a strategic and enriching way to navigate the path toward personal and professional fulfillment.

**The Intrinsic Joy of Goal Pursuit** - The pursuit of a goal itself can provide you with intrinsic satisfaction. As you align actions with aspirations, each step becomes a celebration of progress, offering fulfillment, purpose, and a profound sense of accomplishment on your journey toward personal growth.

1. **Celebrating Milestones:** In pursuing long-term goals, celebrating milestones, no matter how small, is a crucial practice that infuses vibrancy into the journey. Each achieved milestone is a brushstroke of color on the canvas of your evolving narrative. Recognizing and celebrating these moments of progress acknowledges your hard work and fuels motivation for the next steps. It transforms the journey into a series of joyful triumphs, making the path towards your goals fulfilling and a source of continuous inspiration. By savoring the more minor victories, you stay motivated and cultivate a positive mindset that propels you toward more significant accomplishments.

2. **Incorporating Enjoyment:** Infusing enjoyment into pursuing your goals is vital to creating a

sustainable and fulfilling journey. While the destination holds significance, most of your time is spent in the pursuit. Finding joy in the daily steps, regardless of how challenging they may be, transforms the journey from a mere means to an end into a meaningful and enjoyable experience. Cultivating a sense of fulfillment in the present moment enhances resilience, making it easier to navigate obstacles. By incorporating enjoyment into pursuing your goals, you increase your overall well-being and create a positive feedback loop that sustains your motivation and commitment over the long haul.

## The Unfolding Masterpiece: Your Life

Setting personal goals and dreams is akin to becoming the artist of your own life, wielding intentionality as your brush and a blank canvas as your masterpiece. Each goal becomes a purposeful stroke, adding depth and color to the evolving narrative of your existence. It's more than a mere "to-do" list; it's a conscious act crafting a life that resonates with authenticity and purpose.

In self-discovery, your goals are the vibrant hues that bring your authentic self to life. They are not just checkboxes to be checked off but intentional choices that reflect your values, passions, and aspirations. With each goal pursued, your canvas transforms, revealing the layers of your character and the richness of your experiences.

As you navigate this artistic journey, let your goals be the colors that define the contours of your true self. Embrace the process of intentional living, where each stroke contributes to the masterpiece that is your life. In this tapestry of goals and dreams, the authentic essence of who you are emerges, creating a canvas filled with purpose, fulfillment, and the beauty of a life lived with intention.

Accept the skill involved in creating meaningful goals that are time-bound, relevant, quantifiable, and specific. Through the intentional pursuit of your aspirations, you shape the narrative of your life. "Crafting the Palette" invites you to step into the role of artist and muse, orchestrating the colors of your dreams into a harmonious and resonant composition. May your goals be both the brush and colors illuminating the canvas of your unique and fulfilling life.

# CHAPTER 5

## "Weathering the Changes: Building Resilience in Turbulent Times"

### The Spectrum of You: Unveiling Fulfillment in Life's Challenges

In the intricate tapestry of life, resilience is the thread that binds the fabric of personal growth and fulfillment. The acknowledgment that life is an ever-changing landscape lays the foundation for understanding the paramount importance of resilience. This chapter delves into the art of building resilience, recognizing it as a transformative skill that empowers you to weather the storms and positions you to emerge from adversity with newfound strength.

Resilience is the ability to endure challenges and the art of navigating through turbulent times with a spirit that refuses to break. It involves cultivating inner strength, adaptability, and a mindset that views setbacks as opportunities. By embracing resilience, you not only withstand the unpredictable nature of life but also use challenges as catalysts for personal development.

The journey toward personal fulfillment is not immune to storms, setbacks, and uncertainties. However, the art of building resilience enables you to navigate these storms with grace and tenacity. It transforms difficulties into stepping stones, fostering a continuous evolution toward your true potential. In the ebb and flow of life, resilience becomes the compass that guides you through adversity, allowing you to emerge on the other side stronger, wiser, and armed for the journey ahead. The art of building resilience is, therefore, an indispensable and transformative skill that propels you forward on the path toward enduring personal fulfillment.

**Understanding Resilience** – Recognizing resilience as a dynamic attribute formed by adaptive behaviors, emotional coping mechanisms, and mental attitudes is essential to understanding resilience. It's the ability to recover, adjust, and face difficulties without losing your wellbeing.

1. **Definition of Resilience:** The ability to rise above adversity, adjust to changes, and bear suffering with courage is the precise definition of resilience.

It's not about avoiding problems; rather, it's about learning how to overcome them and keep your mental and emotional health. The art of turning adversity into strength is resilience. It's the capacity to overcome obstacles, bear suffering with courage, and preserve wellbeing, demonstrating the ability to bounce back and adjust.

2. **The Dynamic Nature of Resilience:** Rather of being a fixed characteristic, resilience is a dynamic ability that may be enhanced with practice. Its dynamic quality highlights its potential for expansion and improvement, illustrating a never-ending process of strength-building. It combines mental attitudes, emotional strategies, and adaptive behaviors.

   A. Mental attitudes encompass the mindset and beliefs that shape responses to challenges.

   B. Emotional strategies involve regulating and understanding emotions for effective coping.

   C. Adaptive behaviors denote flexible actions that facilitate resilience by navigating difficulties with versatility and growth-oriented approaches.

**The Resilient Mindset** - Through the lens of a resilient attitude, obstacles are seen as chances for personal development. Strong optimism, flexibility, and an embrace of change serve as the cornerstones for overcoming adversity with courage and strength.

1. **Optimism and Positivity:** Cultivate an optimistic mindset that sees challenges as opportunities for growth. Embrace positivity, even in the face of adversity. This mindset shift is the foundation for building resilience. Developing a positive outlook turns obstacles into chances for personal development. Resilience is based on accepting optimism despite hardship. This change in viewpoint gives you the ability to approach challenges constructively, which builds resilience and adaptability.

2. **Acceptance of Change:** Accepting change as a normal aspect of life is a necessary component of resilience. Change should be viewed with an open mind and a readiness to adapt, not with resistance or dread. Accepting change as a constant makes it possible to respond to obstacles with greater resilience. The foundation of resilience is acknowledging change as a necessary part of life. Accepting change with an open mind and a readiness to adjust makes you more resilient to setbacks and turns it from a cause for fear to one of opportunity for development and fortitude.

**Strategies for Building Resilience** – This multifaceted approach enhances adaptability and strength, equipping you to navigate challenges with resilience and a positive outlook. It involves developing problem-solving skills, cultivating emotional intelligence, nurturing social connections, and practicing mindfulness, which fosters adaptability and strength in adversity.

1. **Developing Problem-Solving Skills:** Having a problem-solving mindset when faced with adversity is a key component of resilience. Dividing difficult problems into doable steps and concentrating on workable answers are important. Strong problem-solving abilities make you more resilient to barriers and difficulties. Proficiency in these techniques strengthens your resilience by equipping you with the means to face and overcome hardships. By developing this skill, you give yourself the power to face obstacles with confidence and adaptability.

2. **Cultivating Emotional Intelligence:** One of the main elements of resilience is emotional intelligence. Learn to acknowledge and control your own feelings while cultivating empathy for others. Effectively managing these responses increases the emotional resilience required to overcome obstacles. Gaining emotional intelligence strengthens the emotional fortitude needed to weather challenges, promoting flexibility and a strong reaction to misfortune.

3. **Creating a Support Network:** A strong, supportive network is a cornerstone of resilience. Cultivate

relationships with friends, family, and mentors who provide emotional support, guidance, and encouragement during challenging times. These elements become crucial pillars during difficult periods, fostering strength and adaptability.

4. **Mindfulness and Stress Management:** To manage stress and enhance resilience, incorporate mindfulness practices into your daily routine. Mindfulness allows you to stay present, manage your stress reaction, and build mental fortitude. By promoting present-moment awareness, it aids in stress management and cultivates psychological strength. It equips you with the tools to navigate challenges with clarity, focus, and resilience.

**Adapting to Change** - Getting used to change is a dynamic process that involves accepting that life will inevitably fluctuate. It involves cultivating flexibility, open-mindedness, and a willingness to evolve, enabling you to navigate uncertainties with resilience and a growth-oriented mindset.

1. **Flexibility and Adaptability:** Resilience is necessary in order to adjust to shifting conditions. The secret to managing life's curves is flexibility and adaptability. Growth-oriented responses and resilience are fostered by being open to change and adapting to changing circumstances. Develop and nurture flexibility in your thinking and behavior. Especially when faced with unforeseen obstacles,

be willing to modify your ideas and tactics as necessary.

2. **Learning from Setbacks:** See failures as a chance for development and learning. Instead of moping about mistakes, examine what went wrong, draw lessons, and use them in your next attempts. Resilience is characterized by the capacity to grow and learn from setbacks. Every obstacle turns into a teaching opportunity, providing knowledge that fortifies resilience and advances continuous personal growth.

## Personal Reflection Exercise: The Resilience Journal

Create a resilience journal to document your experiences during challenging times. Reflect on how you responded, the strategies that worked, and areas of opportunity for change. This journal is valuable for understanding your resilience patterns and evolving techniques.

**Here are the elements you can include in a Resilience Journal:**

1. **Date and Situation:** Record the date and briefly describe the challenging situation you are facing. Providing context allows for a more detailed reflection.

2. **Emotional Responses:** Reflect on your emotional responses to the challenging situation. Acknowledge and express the emotions you experienced, from initial reactions to evolving feelings.

3. **Thoughts and Perceptions:** Document your thoughts and perceptions during the challenging times. Explore any automatic negative thoughts and consider how they influenced your emotional state.

4. **Coping Strategies Used:** Identify and describe the coping strategies you employed. Include both immediate responses and long-term strategies. Consider whether these strategies were effective in alleviating stress.

5. **Positive Aspects:** Note any positive aspects or unexpected outcomes that emerged from the challenging situation. This process can help you develop a positive mindset and recognize silver linings.

6. **Areas for Improvement:** Reflect on areas where you believe you could improve your resilience. Consider whether there were moments when you felt overwhelmed or where your coping strategies fell short.

7. **Support Systems:** Document the support systems you utilized: friends, family, mentors, or

professional help. Acknowledge the importance of a strong support network in building resilience.

8. **Lessons Learned:** Identify and articulate the lessons you learned from the challenging experience. Reflect on how these lessons can contribute to your personal growth and future resilience.

9. **Gratitude Journaling:** Include a section for expressing gratitude. Recognize the positive aspects of your life, relationships, or personal strengths that you are thankful for. Gratitude can contribute to resilience.

10. **Self-Compassion:** Practice self-compassion by acknowledging your efforts and accepting imperfections. Write down words of encouragement and self-compassionate statements to foster a positive self-image.

11. **Goal Setting for Resilience:** Set specific goals related to building resilience. Outline steps and actions you can take to enhance your ability to cope with challenges in the future.

12. **Visualization Exercises:** Include visualization exercises to imagine positive outcomes or envision yourself successfully navigating future challenges. Visualization can be a powerful tool for building mental resilience.

13. **Reflection Prompts:** Integrate reflection prompts that encourage deeper analysis. These could include

questions about your mindset, the effectiveness of your coping mechanisms, and areas for personal growth.

14. **Progress Tracking:** Regularly review and track your progress over time. Compare your responses and strategies across different challenging situations to observe patterns and changes in your resilience journey.

Incorporating these elements into your resilience journal creates a comprehensive and personalized tool for self-discovery and growth. The journal becomes a dynamic resource for understanding your resilience patterns, evolving techniques, and navigating future challenges with increased strength and adaptability.

## Embracing Self-Compassion

1. **Kindness to Yourself:** Practice self-compassion during difficult times. Treat yourself with the same kindness and understanding you would offer anyone facing challenges. Acknowledge your efforts and progress, even if the outcomes are unexpected. Kindness to yourself is a pillar of resilience. Here are some ways to show yourself kindness.

    A. **Self-Encouragement:** Offer yourself positive affirmations and words of encouragement, fostering a supportive inner dialogue during challenging moments.

B. **Self-Care Rituals:** Prioritize activities that nourish your well-being, such as exercise, adequate sleep, and moments of relaxation, demonstrating care for your physical and mental health.

C. **Setting Boundaries:** Establish and uphold healthy boundaries to protect your time and energy, prioritize your needs, and avoid unnecessary stress.

D. **Celebrate Achievements:** Acknowledge and celebrate your accomplishments, regardless of size, recognizing your efforts and reinforcing a positive mindset.

E. **Mindful Reflection:** Engage in self-reflection without judgment. This will allow you to understand and accept your emotions and experiences, promoting inner peace and self-awareness.

2. **Balancing Realism and Optimism:** Maintain a realistic perspective while fostering optimism. Acknowledge your challenges and cultivate an optimistic belief in your ability to overcome them. Striking a balance between realism and optimism is crucial for building resilience.

A. **Goal Setting:** Set achievable yet challenging goals, acknowledging potential obstacles (realism) while maintaining a positive belief in your capacity to accomplish them (optimism).

B. **Problem-Solving:** Address challenges by realistically assessing the situation and developing optimistic solutions. Recognize limitations while fostering confidence in your problem-solving abilities.

C. **Adaptability:** Embrace change with a realistic understanding of its inevitability and an optimistic attitude that views change as an opportunity for growth and new possibilities.

D. **Self-Talk:** Maintain a balanced internal dialogue by acknowledging difficulties (realism) and encouraging yourself with optimistic and empowering affirmations (optimism).

E. **Reflecting on Progress:** Realistically assess your current situation and challenges while fostering optimism by reflecting on the progress you've made and envisioning positive outcomes in the future.

**Resilience in the Face of Adversity** - Resilience in the face of adversity is the unwavering strength to navigate challenges, adapt, and emerge stronger, guided by optimism and determination.

1. **Loss and Grief:** Resilience is most tested during periods of loss and grief. Understanding that grieving is a natural process and resilience involves navigating these emotions while gradually adapting to the new reality. Seek support and allow yourself the time and space to heal.

**Here are some ideas to help with the healing process:**

A. **Seek Support:** Connect with friends, family, or a support group to share your feelings and receive emotional support. Having a strong support network is crucial during times of grief.

B. **Professional Guidance:** Consider seeking help from a counselor or therapist who specializes in grief. Professional guidance can provide valuable insights and coping strategies tailored to your unique situation.

C. **Express Emotions:** Allow yourself to feel and express the range of emotions associated with grief. Whether through journaling, art, or conversations, expressing emotions is a vital part of the healing process.

D. **Create Rituals:** Establish rituals or practices that honor the memory of what's lost. This could be a simple daily ritual or a special event dedicated to commemorating the significance of what or who is no longer present.

E. **Focus on Self-Care:** Prioritize self-care activities that promote physical, emotional, and mental well-being. This includes proper nutrition, exercise, adequate sleep, and engaging in activities that bring comfort and solace.

F. **Set Realistic Expectations:** Understand that each individual's grieving process is unique, and healing takes time. Set realistic expectations for yourself, allowing the necessary space and patience to adapt to the changed reality.

G. **Connect with Others Who Have Experienced Similar Loss:** Joining a support group with individuals who have experienced similar loss can provide a sense of understanding and shared experiences, reducing feelings of isolation.

H. **Embrace Moments of Joy:** Finding moments of joy and gratitude is essential while grieving. These moments don't diminish the pain but contribute to a more balanced emotional experience.

I. **Memorialize in a Meaningful Way:** Create a memorial or tribute that holds personal significance. This could involve planting a tree, creating a scrapbook, or participating in activities that symbolize the positive aspects of the person or thing that's been lost.

J. **Practice Patience:** Recognize that healing is a gradual process, and there is no specific timeline for overcoming grief. Be patient with yourself and allow the emotions to unfold naturally, understanding that resilience is built over time.

2. **Maintaining a Sense of Purpose:** A sense of purpose is a powerful source of resilience. During challenging times, reconnect with your values and aspirations. A clear understanding of purpose provides motivation and direction, guiding you through adversity.

**Here are some ideas to help with finding a sense of purpose:**

A. **Reflect on Core Values:** Take time to reflect on your core values and principles. Understanding what truly matters to you provides a foundation for reconnecting with your sense of purpose.

B. **Set Mindful Goals:** Define goals that align with your values and aspirations. Even if small, these goals contribute to a sense of purpose by providing a clear direction and something meaningful to strive for.

C. **Engage in Meaningful Activities:** Participate in activities that bring fulfillment and align with your values. Whether it's volunteering, pursuing a passion, or contributing to a cause, engaging in meaningful actions fosters a sense of purpose.

D. **Connect with Others:** connections with individuals who share similar values or are on a similar journey. Shared experiences and collaborative efforts contribute to a collective sense of purpose, reinforcing motivation and resilience.

E. **Regularly Reassess Goals:** Periodically reassess your goals and aspirations to ensure they remain in harmony with your evolving sense of purpose. Adjusting goals allows for continued alignment with what truly matters to you.

F. **Find Meaning in Adversity:** Look for lessons and meaning in challenging situations. Identifying the purpose or potential for growth in adversity transforms hardships into opportunities for personal development.

G. **Create A Personal Mission Statement:** Develop a personal mission statement that encapsulates your values and aspirations. This concise statement serves as a reminder of your sense of purpose and can guide decision-making during difficult times.

H. **Seek Feedback:** Solicit feedback from trusted friends, mentors, or family members. External perspectives can provide insights into your strengths and areas where your contributions align with a greater purpose.

I. **Cultivate Gratitude:** Practice gratitude by focusing on the positive aspects of your life. Recognizing and appreciating the blessings you have contributes to a sense of purpose and a more resilient mindset.

J. **Adopt a Growth Mindset:** Adopt a growth mindset that sees challenges as opportunities for learning and development. Embracing a mindset of continuous growth contributes to an enduring sense of purpose.

**The Transformative Power of Resilience** - Resilience has the capacity to change hardship into growth by promoting fortitude, insight, and a fresh sense of direction.

1. **Personal Growth and Transformation:** Resilience is not just about enduring difficulties but also

about personal growth and transformation. Your challenges become catalysts for self-discovery, inner strength, and a deepened sense of purpose.

A. **Self-Discovery:** Self-discovery is the process of gaining insight into your true identity, values, and beliefs. It involves exploring your passions, understanding your strengths and weaknesses, and unraveling the layers of your personality shaped by life experiences. Through self-reflection and introspection, you unearth the authentic essence of who you are.

B. **Inner Strength:** Inner strength is the reservoir of resilience and fortitude that resides within. It's the capacity to withstand adversity, overcome challenges, and navigate life's ups and downs with courage and grace. Cultivating inner strength involves developing a positive mindset, managing emotions effectively, and tapping into your innate resilience to face difficulties head-on.

C. **Sense of Purpose:** A sense of purpose is the guiding force that gives your life direction and meaning. It stems from aligning your actions and goals with your core values and passions. When faced with challenges, a strong sense of purpose is a motivational anchor, inspiring you to persevere and contributing to your personal growth. It answers the fundamental question of why you do what you do, providing a compass for your journey of self-discovery and transformation.

2. **Resilience as a Lifelong Skill:** The process of becoming resilient takes a lifetime. As you go through different phases of life, the abilities and mindset you acquire become priceless instruments. It is possible to face uncertainty with greater assurance when you accept resilience as an ongoing process. Like a dynamic travel partner, resilience changes as you do. Over time, you develop coping mechanisms and an adaptive attitude that become valuable assets. When you accept resilience as a continuous process, you gain the ability to face life's uncertainties with increasing self-assurance and flexibility.

**Nurturing Resilience in Daily Life** - Nurturing resilience involves cultivating a positive mindset, building supportive connections, and adapting with grace to challenges, fostering strength and well-being.

1. **Daily Practicing:** Integrate resilience-building practices into your daily life. Whether through mindfulness exercises, maintaining a support network, or setting aside time for self-reflection, daily habits contribute to the cumulative strength of your resilience.

2. **Seeking Professional Support:** In times of significant challenges, consider seeking professional support. Therapists, counselors, or coaches can provide guidance, strategies, and a safe space for processing emotions and building resilience.

**Here are some practices for building resilience that you can integrate into your daily life:**

1. **Mindfulness Meditation:**

    Engage in daily mindfulness meditation to cultivate a present-focused awareness. This practice can help you manage stress, enhance emotional regulation, and build a resilient mindset.

2. **Gratitude Journaling:**

    Keep a gratitude journal where you write down things you are thankful for each day. Focusing on positive aspects fosters a mindset of appreciation and resilience.

3. **Physical Exercise:**

    Incorporate regular physical exercise into your routine. Exercise improves mental health, reduces stress, and increases resilience.

4. **Healthy Sleep Habits:**

    Prioritize quality sleep by establishing consistent sleep patterns. A well-rested mind and body are better equipped to handle challenges and stressors.

5. **Maintain Social Connections:**

    Foster and strengthen social connections. Regularly engage with friends, family, or support groups to build a reliable network contributing to emotional well-being.

6. **Practice Self-Compassion:**

    Cultivate self-compassion by treating yourself with kindness during difficult times. Acknowledge your humanity, understand that everyone faces challenges, and avoid self-judgment.

7. **Set Realistic Goals:**

    Break larger goals into smaller, manageable tasks. Setting realistic and achievable daily or weekly goals builds a sense of accomplishment and confidence in your abilities.

8. **Mindful Breathing Exercises:**

    Incorporate mindful breathing exercises like deep belly breathing to promote relaxation and regulate stress responses. These exercises can be done throughout the day, especially during tense moments.

9. **Seeking Social Support:**

    Actively seek and nurture social support. Share your thoughts and feelings with trusted friends or family members. A robust social support system contributes significantly to resilience.

10. **Reflective Practices:**

    Set aside time for daily reflection. Journaling, self-reflection, or mindfulness practices that encourage introspection can enhance self-awareness and contribute to resilience.

11. **Learn from Adversity:**

    View challenges and obstacles as opportunities for learning and growth. Identify lessons from difficult experiences, focusing on personal strengths and areas for development.

12. **Professional Counseling:**

    When facing significant challenges, consider seeking professional support from therapists, counselors, or coaches. Professional guidance can provide tailored strategies, coping mechanisms, and a safe space for processing emotions.

13. **Cultivate Optimism:**

    Promote an optimistic mindset by focusing on the positive aspects of situations. Use reframing practices from negative thoughts into more positive or constructive perspectives.

14. **Maintain Flexibility:**

    Develop adaptability and flexibility in your approach to challenges. Being open to alternative solutions and adjusting expectations can reduce the impact of unexpected stressors.

15. **Connect with Nature:**

    Spend time outdoors and connect with nature. Exposure to natural environments improves mood, reduces stress, and enhances well-being.

Integrating a combination of these practices into your daily routine creates a holistic approach to building resilience. Consistency and commitment to these habits contribute to the cumulative strength needed to navigate life's challenges with resilience and a positive mindset.

## A Resilient Journey Forward

Navigating life's ever-changing landscape is akin to embarking on a continuous journey where challenges and uncertainties are inevitable. "Weathering the Changes" becomes a profound invitation to approach these challenges not as insurmountable obstacles but as opportunities for cultivating resilience. It's a mindset that acknowledges the storms, the inevitable fluctuations in life, as integral parts of the narrative, each presenting a canvas for the brushstroke of resilience.

In the canvas of life, resilience is not just a reactive force but an active participant, contributing depth and richness to your narrative. The brushstroke adds vibrant colors to your experiences, transforming trials into opportunities for growth and self-discovery. Embracing challenges becomes a deliberate act of artistic expression, where the colors of resilience merge with the darker shades of adversity, creating a masterpiece that tells the story of endurance, adaptability, and strength.

The essence lies in seeing each trial not as a setback but as a canvas for resilience, a space where the most vibrant colors within you can shine through. With a resilient mindset, challenges become transformative moments, revealing the enduring strength that resides within, waiting to be discovered. As you weather the changes, may you not only withstand the storms but emerge from them with a canvas of personal growth and fulfillment, a testament to the beautiful and intricate artwork that resilience can create in the face of life's fluctuations.

In the canvas of life, resilience becomes the brushstroke that adds depth and richness to your narrative. May you embrace the challenges as opportunities, knowing that each trial is a canvas for resilience, a testament to the vibrant colors within you. As you weather the changes, may you discover the enduring strength that transforms adversity into a masterpiece of personal growth and fulfillment.

# CHAPTER 6

# "Rainbow Mindset: Shifting Perspectives for Positivity"

## Resilient Hues: Creating Your Canvas of Personal Growth

In the kaleidoscope of life, the lens through which we perceive our experiences shapes the vibrant spectrum of our journey. The exploration of perspective in this chapter illuminates the transformative power it holds – a prism that refracts life's moments into an array of colors. Shifting perspective becomes an art, much like adjusting the focus of a camera lens, allowing us to see the beauty and possibilities inherent in every situation.

Like a rainbow emerging after the storm, cultivating a positive mindset acts as a spark, infusing vibrancy into our path. It's not about denying the challenges or difficulties but viewing them through a lens that highlights resilience, growth, and opportunity. A positive mindset becomes the artist's palette, influencing our thoughts, emotions, and actions, ultimately painting a more uplifting and optimistic narrative on the canvas of our lives. In the symphony of experiences, perspective is the conductor, orchestrating a harmonious melody that enhances the beauty of our journey.

**The Impact of Perspective** - Perspective shapes how we perceive and respond to challenges, influencing resilience, growth, and the ability to find opportunities within difficulties.

1. **Definition of Perspective:** The filter through which you see and understand the things that happen in your life is called perspective. It molds your opinions, attitudes, and problem-solving techniques. Adopting a rainbow mindset entails deliberately viewing life from an optimistic perspective, allowing the vibrant colors of positivity to infuse our experiences.

2. **Influence on Well-Being:** The influence of perspective extends beyond mere perception; it significantly impacts overall well-being. A positive outlook can enhance mental and emotional health,

reduce stress, and contribute to a more fulfilling and resilient life. A positive outlook acts as a powerful tonic for mental and emotional health, alleviating tension and contributing to a life that is more fulfilling and resilient in the face of adversity. Consciously embracing an optimistic perspective becomes a transformative practice, painting the canvas of our lives with the hues of positivity and fostering a brighter, more vibrant existence.

**Cultivating a Rainbow Mindset** - Adopting a rainbow mindset involves embracing diverse perspectives, finding beauty in challenges, and fostering resilience through a colorful spectrum of positive outlooks.

1. **Awareness of Thought Patterns:** The first step in cultivating a positive mindset is understanding your thought patterns. Pay attention to the narratives you create about yourself, others, and the events in your life. Identify any recurring negative thought patterns that may be hindering positivity.

2. **The Power of Reframing:** Reframing is the art of consciously changing the way you interpret situations. It involves finding alternatives and more positive perspectives on challenges. For example, viewing setbacks as opportunities for growth or difficulties as temporary hurdles can shift your mindset toward positivity.

**Here are some elements of a Rainbow mindset, focusing on cultivating positivity:**

A. **Awareness of Thought Patterns:**

Beginning a positive change process requires self-awareness. Pay close attention to the narratives you construct about yourself, others, and life events. Determine whether you have any negative thought patterns that are coming up and affecting the way you see things. To start a meaningful change, this self-assessment is essential.

B. **The Power of Reframing:**

One effective strategy for developing a rainbow mindset is reframing. It entails deliberately altering your perspective on events. Look for alternative and more optimistic viewpoints rather than concentrating on negativity. Consider obstacles as teaching moments, obstacles as short-term roadblocks, and setbacks as chances for personal development. Through reframing, you can change your perspective and cultivate a more positive attitude.

C. **Gratitude Practice:**

Make it a habit to express thankfulness every day. Develop a positive outlook on life by recognizing and being grateful for the people, occasions, and experiences that bring you joy and fulfillment.

D. **Mindfulness and Presence:**

Accept mindfulness to maintain present-moment awareness. Being totally present allows you to enjoy the beauty that surrounds you and lessens needless anxiety about the past or the future. Being mindful improves your capacity to concentrate on the advantages of the situation you are in at the moment.

E. **Positive Affirmations:**

Adopt a daily practice of saying encouraging statements to yourself. Make affirmations that boost you and highlight your potential, strengths, and good attributes. Reframing your self-perception and creating a more positive self-image are two benefits of using affirmations.

F. **Solution-Oriented Thinking:**

Adopt a solution-oriented mindset. Instead of dwelling on problems, focus on finding constructive solutions. This approach empowers you to navigate challenges with a proactive and optimistic attitude.

G. **Acts of Kindness:**

Engage in acts of kindness toward yourself and others. Acts of kindness not only contribute to a positive and compassionate environment but also generate a sense of fulfillment and connection.

H. **Positive Social Connections:**

   Surround yourself with positive and supportive people. Cultivating positive social connections uplifts your mood and provides a network of encouragement during challenging times.

I. **Self-Compassion:**

   Allow yourself kindness by treating yourself with compassion and understanding. Acknowledge that everyone faces challenges and be supportive of yourself like you would support a friend.

J. **Celebrating Small Wins:**

   Celebrate small victories and achievements. Celebrating your successes, no matter how minor, contributes to a positive mindset and reinforces the idea that progress is happening.

By incorporating these elements into your outlook, you create a Rainbow mindset that refracts the light of positivity into various facets of your life. This approach encourages a more optimistic interpretation of experiences and fosters resilience in facing challenges.

**Positive Affirmations and Self-Talk** - Constructive statements and optimistic self-talk involve nurturing a supportive inner dialogue, fostering resilience, and empowering oneself with optimistic beliefs and encouragement.

1. **Introduction to Positive Affirmations:** Strong declarations that support self-affirming ideas about your potential are known as positive affirmations. A more optimistic outlook can be attained by altering the way you talk to yourself and introducing affirmations into your daily routine. A transformative journey of self-discovery and empowerment is facilitated by positive assertions. These powerful statements are the incentive for reinforcing constructive beliefs about yourself and your abilities. This invites you to recognize the impact of your inner dialogue and the potential for reshaping your thoughts through intentional and positive self-talk.

2. **Constructive Self-Talk:** Monitor your self-talk for signs of negativity and self-criticism. Transform negative thoughts into constructive ones. For instance, replace thoughts such as "I can't do this" with "I am capable and will take this one step at a time." Positive self-talk is a cornerstone of a rainbow mindset and the call to monitor the statements you say to yourself signifies an essential step toward self-awareness. You can intercept and redirect these thoughts by being attuned to signs of negativity and self-criticism.

Positive self-talk becomes the pillar of a Rainbow mindset, influencing thoughts, emotions, and actions. It's a conscious choice to cultivate an inner dialogue that uplifts and motivates, paving the way for a more optimistic perspective on challenges and opportunities. Through constructive self-talk, you counteract negativity and actively contribute to the vibrancy and richness of your personal narrative, aligning with the principles of the Rainbow mindset.

**Gratitude as a Catalyst for Positivity** - Gratitude acts as a driving force for positivity by cultivating appreciation, shifting focus to blessings, and fostering resilience through a grateful perspective.

1. **Practicing Gratitude:** Gratitude is a formidable force that can shift your focus from what is lacking to what is abundant in your life. Practicing gratitude is akin to unlocking a powerful drive that can transform your perspective from focusing on what you don't have to acknowledging what you do have. Including a daily gratitude routine turns it into a ritual of introspection, a time to intentionally acknowledge and value the good events that have happened in your day. This habitual exercise fosters a mindset of appreciation and positivity, gradually shaping the lens through which you view the world.

2. **The Ripple Effect of Gratitude:** Cultivating gratitude has a ripple effect on your perspective. When you acknowledge and appreciate the positive elements in your life, your outlook becomes more optimistic. This upbeat viewpoint permeates your interactions, relationships, and overall well-being. The practice of gratitude acts as a catalyst, creating a harmonious resonance that uplifts your spirit and contributes to a constructive atmosphere in your interactions with others. The ripple effect is a testament to the profound impact that a simple daily practice of gratitude can have on nurturing a more optimistic and fulfilling life.

**Embracing a Growth Mindset** - A growth mindset involves viewing challenges as opportunities for learning, fostering resilience, and nurturing a belief in your ability to develop new skills and adapt to change.

1. **Definition of a Growth Mindset:** Having a progressive attitude entails viewing obstacles and failures as chances for development; and adopting a growth mentality enables you to approach challenges with fortitude and an optimistic outlook. It's a potent paradigm that radically alters how you tackle the challenges of life. It's more than simply a way of thinking; it's a philosophy that welcomes adversity with fortitude and optimism.

2. **Embracing Challenges:** Rather than viewing obstacles with fear or avoidance, this mindset offers the opportunity to perceive challenges as essential stepping stones on the journey toward personal development. This mindset hinges on the belief that abilities are not fixed but can be developed and strengthened through persistent efforts and perseverance.

In cultivating a growth mindset, you can navigate challenges more effectively and foster a sense of empowerment and adaptability. It's an invitation to view setbacks not as roadblocks but as opportunities to refine skills, deepen understanding, and ultimately evolve into a more capable and resilient version of yourself. The growth mindset is not just a lens through which challenges are viewed; it's a transformative approach that empowers you to actively engage with difficulties, recognizing them as integral elements in the continuous journey of self-improvement and development.

## Personal Reflection Exercise: Positive Journaling

Initiate a positive journaling practice to document moments of joy, achievement, and gratitude. Regularly revisit your entries to reinforce positive experiences. Positive journaling is a tangible reminder of the abundance of positivity in your life.

**Here are some elements to include as you reflect on your progress:**

1. **Gratitude Entries:**

    Begin each journaling session by expressing gratitude. List things you are thankful for, both big and small. Focusing on appreciation and gratitude sets a positive tone for your reflections.

2. **Joyful Moments:**

    Document moments of joy and happiness. These could be simple pleasures, accomplishments, or moments that brought a smile to your face. Recording these instances reinforces the positivity in your life.

3. **Achievements and Milestones:**

    Note down your achievements and milestones, even if they seem minor. Recognizing and celebrating your accomplishments contributes to a sense of fulfillment and motivation.

4. **Positive Affirmations:**

    Include positive affirmations relevant to your experiences. Affirmations can reinforce positive beliefs about yourself and your capabilities, fostering a more positive self-perception.

5. **Reflections on Challenges:**

    Reflect on challenges you've faced and overcome. Write about the lessons you learned and the personal growth you achieved through the adversity. This activity adds a resilience component to your positive journaling.

6. **Random Acts of Kindness:**

    Record instances where you either performed or received random acts of kindness. Kindness contributes to positive interactions and fosters a sense of connection and community.

7. **Surprise and Delight:**

    Document moments that pleasantly surprised or delighted you. These unexpected positive experiences can serve as reminders of the beauty in everyday life.

8. **Quotes and Inspirations:**

    Include inspirational quotes or passages that resonate with you. These can serve as motivational reminders and contribute to a positive mindset.

9. **Personal Growth Reflections:**

    Reflect on your growth journey. Write about the skills you've developed, the challenges you've conquered, and the person you are becoming.

This reflection reinforces a sense of continuous improvement.

10. **Visualization Exercises:**

    Incorporate visualization exercises in your positive journaling—picture future successes and positive outcomes, reinforcing a forward-looking and optimistic mindset.

11. **Highlighting Connections:**

    Acknowledge and celebrate positive connections with others. Include moments of shared joy, support, and camaraderie.

12. **Weekly or Monthly Summaries:**

    Periodically, provide a summary of positive highlights for the week or month. This summary allows for a holistic view of the positivity in your life over time.

Positive journaling is a tangible and personalized reminder of the abundance of positivity in your life. Rereading these posts on a regular basis helps to cultivate a mindset that emphasizes acknowledging and valuing the good events that have happened to you and reinforces your positive experiences.

## Positivity in Interactions and Relationships

1. **Positive Communication:** The way you communicate with yourself as well as others shapes your reality. Offer encouragement, express appreciation, and create an environment that fosters positivity. Positive communication is the cornerstone of constructing a reality infused with optimism and empowerment. The language we use, internally and externally, is pivotal in shaping our perception of the world. Engaging in positive and uplifting communication involves consciously choosing words that inspire and motivate, both in our self-talk and interactions with others. Offering encouragement and expressing appreciation for our achievements and the accomplishments of those around us creates a nurturing environment that fosters positivity.

2. **Building Positive Relationships:** Surround yourself with individuals who contribute to a positive atmosphere. Cultivate relationships that uplift, support, and share in your journey towards personal fulfillment. Supportive connections enhance the overall positivity in your life. Building positive relationships is an extension of this intentional communication. Surrounding yourself with people who contribute to a positive atmosphere becomes a strategic decision in the pursuit of personal fulfillment.

The energy and encouragement derived from these relationships create a harmonious backdrop against which we can navigate the complexities of life, promoting resilience, fulfillment, and a shared sense of purpose.

## Overcoming Negativity Bias

1. **Understanding Negativity Bias:** Negativity bias is the tendency of the mind to focus more on negative experiences than positive ones. Awareness of this bias is crucial for consciously shifting your perspective towards positivity and cultivating a positive mindset. This bias has evolutionary roots, where early humans needed to prioritize potential threats for survival. However, this bias can lead to an unbalanced perception of reality.

2. **Balancing Feedback:** When faced with feedback or criticism, strive for a balanced perspective. Acknowledge areas for improvement while also recognizing your strengths and achievements. Being aware of negativity bias is crucial for intentional and conscious perspective shifts. It's an acknowledgment that your mind may naturally gravitate towards negative thoughts or experiences and that deliberate effort is required to counteract this tendency. By recognizing your own negativity bias, you can actively redirect your attention toward the positive aspects of your experiences, fostering

a more optimistic outlook. Balancing feedback then becomes a conscious practice in fostering a healthier and more well-adjusted mindset.

## The Resilience-Positivity Loop

1. **Interconnected Nature of Resilience and Positivity:** Resilience and positivity are interconnected elements of personal growth. Together, they form a reinforcing loop that contributes to your general happiness. A positive mindset is crucial for enhancing resilience, creating a mental framework that views adversity as opportunities for growth rather than roadblocks on your journey. In turn, resilience reinforces a positive outlook by enabling you to bounce back from setbacks, learn from experiences, and cultivate a sense of inner strength. This reciprocal relationship forms a fortifying sphere that contributes significantly to your overall well-being. When faced with adversity, embracing a rainbow mindset becomes a tangible demonstration of resilience.

2. **Positivity in the Face of Adversity:** Embracing a rainbow mindset during challenging times is a testament to your resilience. Positivity allows you to navigate difficulties with grace and becomes a testament to your ability to find solutions, maintain hope, and exhibit unwavering strength even when confronted with life's complexities.

The fusion of resilience and positivity creates a powerful synergy, enabling you to weather the storms of life and emerge from them with newfound strength and optimism. This dynamic duo becomes integral to the personal growth journey, shaping a narrative and emphasizing the transformative potential within every challenge and the enduring capacity for positivity even in adversity.

## Integrating Positivity into Daily Life

1. **Mindful Living:** Is a foundational practice for cultivating and sustaining a positive mindset. Practicing mindfulness involves staying fully present in each moment, observing thoughts without judgment, and consciously choosing positive perspectives. This intentional presence allows you to disengage from automatic negative thought patterns and actively shape your mindset towards positivity. Mindful living fosters a continual connection with the present, emphasizing the richness of each moment and promoting a more optimistic and appreciative outlook on life. In short, mindful living nurtures a constant bond with the present, promoting positivity.

2. **Joyful Awareness:** Find activities that bring you joy and contribute to an overall sense of fulfillment. These activities contribute to a positive mindset. Pursuing hobbies, spending time with nature or a furry friend, or connecting with loved ones are

avenues to find joy. Prioritize moments that uplift your spirits and bring you the most happiness. Joyful awareness is another critical element and involves actively seeking and engaging in activities that bring joy and contribute to an overall sense of fulfillment. Identifying and prioritizing activities that uplift your spirits and bring genuine happiness is vital for maintaining a positive mindset. By consciously incorporating joyful activities into daily life, you infuse your experiences with happiness and create a proactive approach to maintaining a positive and fulfilling mindset.

## ■ Painting Your Rainbow Mindset

As you journey towards personal fulfillment, the colors of your mindset play a crucial role in shaping the landscape of your experiences. "Rainbow Mindset" encourages you to embrace the transformative power of positive perspectives, reframing challenges as opportunities and infusing your life with the vibrancy of gratitude, growth, and resilience.

When you set out on the path to personal fulfillment, think of your attitude as the brush with which you will paint the scenes of your encounters. The notion of a "Rainbow Mindset" serves as a call to acknowledge the transforming potential innate in embracing optimistic viewpoints. It is a deliberate decision to reinterpret obstacles as chances for education and development, bringing vivid colors of thankfulness, ongoing improvement, and unflinching fortitude into your life.

Embracing a Rainbow Mindset is not just a shift in thinking; it's an active participation in co-creating your narrative. Each positive perspective becomes a brushstroke that adds depth and richness to the canvas of your life. The colors of gratitude allow you to appreciate the beauty in every moment, fostering a sense of abundance. The hues of growth propel you forward, encouraging a mindset that sees adversity as stepping stones rather than obstacles. The shades of resilience fortify your spirit, enabling you to gracefully navigate life.

In the canvas of your experiences, the Rainbow Mindset becomes a dynamic and ever-evolving masterpiece. It's a commitment to finding joy in the journey, celebrating the endless possibilities, and embracing the inherent beauty of every challenge. As you wield the brush of positivity, you actively contribute to shaping a life that reflects the brilliance of your true self, creating a vibrant and fulfilling narrative.

You are the artist, and positivity is the palette. May you paint your Rainbow Mindset with intention, choosing the hues of optimism, gratitude, and resilience. As you shift perspective towards positivity, may your journey be adorned with the brilliance of a life well-lived, colored by the richness of your unique and fulfilling experiences.

# CHAPTER 7

# "Painting Your Path: Setting Goals and Creating a Vision"

## Unveiling Your Potential: Cultivating Strengths and Talents

In the hunt for personal fulfillment, each person possesses unique strengths and talents waiting to be discovered and developed. This chapter explores the transformative journey of identifying, nurturing, and leveraging your innate abilities. Developing your strengths and talents enriches your life and propels you toward a more profound sense of purpose and fulfillment.

**Recognizing Strengths and Talents** - Recognizing strengths and talents involves acknowledging personal capabilities, enhancing self-awareness, and leveraging these attributes to navigate challenges and build resilience.

1. **Understanding Strengths:** Strengths are inherent qualities and capabilities that come naturally to you. When utilized appropriately, they are the attributes that contribute to your success, satisfaction, and overall well-being. Acknowledging your strengths involves self-awareness and a keen observation of your abilities.

2. **Defining Talents:** Talents go beyond skills; they are innate abilities that you effortlessly excel in. While skills can be learned, talents are intrinsic. Identifying your abilities involves recognizing areas where you demonstrate exceptional ability and passion. It refers to your innate capabilities, aptitudes, or natural skills that you possess, often contributing to your exceptional performance or achievement in specific areas.

**The Power of Self-Discovery** - The power of self-discovery lies in uncovering your values, passions, and strengths, paving the way for authenticity, fulfillment, and personal growth.

1. **Self-Reflective Practices:** Begin the journey of unveiling your potential through self-reflective practices. Journaling, meditation, and introspection create a sacred space to explore your experiences, preferences, and the activities that bring you joy.

Through these deliberate practices self-awareness and personal growth is promoted.

2. **Feedback and Observations:** Seek feedback from trusted friends, colleagues, and mentors. Others often provide valuable insights into your strengths and talents that may need to be more apparent. Pay attention to patterns in the feedback and observe moments where you feel most engaged and fulfilled. Feedback from trusted sources illuminates strengths and talents, offering valuable insights. Observe moments of fulfillment and engagement to identify areas where your unique abilities shine.

**Mapping Your Strengths and Talents** - Mapping strengths and talents involves identifying and acknowledging your unique qualities. It's a self-discovery journey that reveals your inherent abilities, fostering personal and professional growth.

1. **Strengths Assessment:** Consider utilizing strengths assessment tools to understand your innate strengths more comprehensively. These tools can provide structured insights into your unique abilities, aiding a more thorough understanding of them. They can guide self-awareness and empower the intentional leveraging of your strengths for personal and professional success. A wide variety of Strength Assessment Tools can be found

online and can provide insights into your unique capabilities.

2. **Talent Exploration:** Talent exploration involves diverse activities to uncover innate abilities. Through experimentation, you discern areas where your unique talents flourish, leading to a more fulfilling and purposeful life. Engage in activities across various domains to explore and identify your talents. Experimentation allows you to discover areas where you naturally excel and feel fulfilled.

**Here are some ways for you to Map your strengths and talents:**

1. **Talent Exploration Through Hobbies:**

    **Description:** Engaging in various hobbies allows you to experiment with different skills and activities. Pay attention to those that resonate with you and where you feel a natural inclination or passion.

    **Example:** Trying photography, painting, coding, or playing a musical instrument might help you discover talents and passions you weren't previously unaware of.

2. **Cross-Functional Projects at Work:**

   **Description:** Participating in cross-functional projects at your workplace allows you to explore different aspects of your skill set. You can discover strengths that may not be evident in your day-to-day tasks.

   **Example:** If you usually work in a technical role, volunteering for a project involving marketing or customer service collaboration can help you identify additional talents like communication or interpersonal skills.

3. **Skill-building Workshops:**

   **Description:** Attend workshops or courses that cover a range of skills. This approach allows you to experiment with various abilities and identify areas where you excel.

   **Example:** Participating in a leadership development workshop might reveal strong organizational or motivational skills you didn't know you had.

4. **Volunteer Opportunities:**

   **Description:** Volunteering for different causes exposes you to diverse tasks and responsibilities. It provides a chance to identify strengths that manifest in a service-oriented context.

> **Example:** Volunteering at a community event might unveil leadership, communication, or problem-solving skills you can develop further.

These examples showcase the importance of intentional exploration and assessment in identifying strengths and talents. Combining formal assessments with real-world experiences allows for a comprehensive understanding of your capabilities, leading to informed decisions in personal and professional pursuits.

**Fostering a Growth Mindset** - Fostering a growth mindset involves embracing challenges, persisting through setbacks, and seeing effort as a path to mastery and continuous improvement.

1. **Embracing a Growth Mindset:** As stated above, cultivating a growth mindset allows you to view abilities as malleable tools to be developed over time. It opens doors to continual development. Embracing challenges and viewing efforts as a path to improvement enhances your capacity to nurture and expand your strengths and talents.

2. **Learning and Skill Development:** Recognize that talents can be further enhanced through continuous learning and skill development. Talents flourish with ongoing education and competence maturity. Identifying areas for growth and investing effort in acquiring complementary skills amplifies

the expression of your innate abilities. Take time to identify areas where you want to grow and invest time and effort in acquiring new skills that complement your innate abilities.

Developing a growth mindset and committing to continuous learning and skill development are powerful personal growth strategies. Embracing a growth mindset not only fosters adaptability but also cultivates resilience in the face of challenges. It encourages you to view setbacks as avenues for knowledge and to persist in your efforts, ultimately leading to greater personal and professional fulfillment.

**Here are examples that illustrate these concepts:**

1. **Online Courses and Workshops:**

    **Description:** Enroll in online courses or workshops that align with your interests and goals. You can find various online or in-person courses, allowing you to develop or deepen new skills.

    **Example:** If you want to enhance your communication skills, you might take a course on the elements of effective communication.

2. **Professional Certifications:**

    **Description:** Pursue industry-recognized certifications to validate your expertise in a specific area. Certifications enhance your knowledge and demonstrate a commitment to ongoing professional development.

**Example:** A certification in such fields as nursing, mechanics, teaching or plumbing can open new avenues for career growth.

3. **Book Clubs and Reading Lists:**

    **Description:** Join a book club or create a reading list on topics that expand your knowledge and skills. Reading relevant literature exposes you to different perspectives and insights.

    **Example:** If you›re interested in cooking, reading books by renowned chefs or exploring the history of cooking other cultures can contribute to your growth.

4. **Cross-Functional Projects:**

    **Description:** Seek opportunities to volunteer for projects that require collaboration with others. This provides a platform for skill development outside your comfort zone.

    **Example:** Participating in projects involving marketing, sales, and product development can improve your communication, teamwork, and problem-solving skills.

5. **Language Learning Apps:**

   **Description:** Use language learning apps to acquire proficiency in a new language. Learning a new language broadens your communication skills and enhances cognitive abilities.

   **Example:** Apps like Duolingo or Rosetta Stone can help you develop language skills, foster cultural understanding, and open doors to new opportunities.

6. **Networking Events and Conferences:**

   **Description:** Attend networking events and conferences related to your area of interest. Engaging with others, attending workshops, and participating in discussions and forums provide valuable insights and opportunities for skill development.

   **Example:** A conference on computing may offer workshops on the latest trends, allowing you to enhance your skills in this rapidly evolving field.

7. **Mentorship Programs:**

   **Description:** Seek mentorship from experienced individuals. A mentor can guide, share knowledge, and help you develop your skills.

   **Example:** As you aspire for personal growth, a mentorship program can provide insights into self-awareness, decision-making, and strategic thinking.

These examples highlight the diversity of opportunities available for learning and skill development. Embracing a growth mindset involves actively seeking and capitalizing on these opportunities, recognizing that every challenge and effort contributes to personal improvement.

**Integration of Strengths into Goals** - Incorporating your strengths seamlessly into your goals allows you to leverage them as powerful assets. Aligning your pursuits with your innate abilities enhances your effectiveness and fulfillment.

1. **Aligning Strengths with Goals:** Link your abilities and strengths to your overarching life objectives. Think about the ways in which your natural abilities can support you in achieving your goals. When objectives and strengths are in line, an interaction is created that helps you succeed.

    Reaching your goals and matching your skills together is like grabbing hold of a strong current that drives you toward achievement in a genuine and satisfying way. A synergy is created that multiplies your efforts when you connect your intrinsic strengths with your larger life goals. Think of your strengths as guiding lights that shine down on your path, giving you direction and clarity. Finding the ways in which your special abilities support you in achieving your goals gives your path direction and intentionality.

2. **Setting Strengths-Based Goals:** Formulate goals that leverage your strengths. Instead of focusing solely on addressing weaknesses, center your goals around amplifying and applying your strengths in various areas of your life.

Setting strengths-based goals is a transformative approach that shifts the focus from weaknesses to strengths. By centering your goals around leveraging and expanding your natural assets, you play to your natural capabilities and cultivate a sense of empowerment. These goals become more than tasks; they are strategic steps aligned with your inherent talents, creating a harmonious and effective personal and professional growth strategy. As you navigate challenges and celebrate achievements, your strengths serve as reliable companions, guiding you toward success with confidence and authenticity.

**The Intersection of Passion and Proficiency** - Passion intersects with proficiency, creating a harmonious interaction. Aligning what you love with your inherent skills fosters excellence and genuine fulfillment in your endeavors.

1. **Identifying Passion Areas:** Passion fuels the cultivation of strength. Determine which subjects

excite you and are consistent with your beliefs. Integrating passion into your pursuits enhances your commitment and dedication.

Identifying areas where you are most passionate is a crucial step in cultivating strength and fulfillment. Passion is a powerful motivator, infusing your pursuits with enthusiasm and sustaining your commitment over the long term. When you identify areas that genuinely ignite your desire and align with your values, your efforts become more than tasks—they become meaningful expressions of your authentic self. Integrating passion into your pursuits enhances your dedication and transforms challenges into opportunities for growth and self-discovery.

2. **Balancing Passion and Proficiency:** While passion is essential, balancing it with proficiency ensures a comprehensive approach. Balancing passion with proficiency means recognizing your natural talents and strengths and actively developing them. Strengthening your proficiency in areas where you are naturally talented allows your desire to manifest as excellence. This balance creates a dynamic interplay where your passion fuels your commitment, and your proficiency ensures that your efforts are grounded in skill and competence.

In pursuing your personal goals, the harmony between passion and proficiency leads to a fulfilling and sustainable journey. It transforms your endeavors into a labor of love, where the joy of pursuing what you love is complemented by the satisfaction of doing it well. This holistic approach not only maximizes your impact but also fosters a sense of alignment with your true self, creating a path that is both purposeful and rewarding.

**Creating a Strengths-Based Plan** - Foster a strengths-based plan by leveraging your innate abilities. Align goals with your strengths, maximizing effectiveness and ensuring a fulfilling journey toward personal and professional achievements.

1. **Setting Strategic Objectives:** Develop plans that outlines strategic objectives for cultivating your innate abilities. Define specific actions and milestones that align with your strengths and contribute to your growth.

2. **Regular Self-Assessment:** Regularly assess your progress in cultivating your strengths. Consider your strengths and how they have been applied in various situations and their impact. Adjust your plan as needed to align with your evolving goals.

Strength-based planning involves a thoughtful and intentional approach to personal and professional development, focusing on leveraging and cultivating innate abilities. It empowers individuals to identify their unique talents and capitalize on them effectively. By aligning goals with innate strengths, you can optimize your performance, enhance satisfaction, and achieve greater success in both your personal and professional endeavors.

**Here are some key elements of strength-based planning:**

1. **Identification of Core Strengths:**

    **Description:** Begin by identifying your core strengths and innate abilities. This involves self-reflection, feedback from others, and potentially utilizing strengths assessment tools.

    **Application:** Recognizing your key strengths forms the foundation for strategic planning, ensuring that your efforts align with your natural capabilities.

2. **Strategic Objective Development:**

    **Description:** Develop clear and specific strategic objectives that center around cultivating and applying your strengths. These objectives should be aligned with your broader goals.

    **Application:** By setting objectives, you create a roadmap that guides your actions and milestones, ensuring a targeted and purposeful approach to developing your innate abilities.

3. **Actionable Steps and Milestones:**

   **Description:** Break down each strategic objective into actionable steps and milestones. Define specific tasks and deadlines that contribute to achieving your strengths-based goals.

   **Application:** Actionable steps clarify how to implement your plan, making it more manageable and allowing for measurable progress.

4. **Integration with Life Goals:**

   **Description:** Ensure your strengths-based plan integrates with your broader life goals. Consider how cultivating specific strengths aligns with your overall personal fulfillment vision.

   **Application:** This integration adds a layer of purpose to your plan, ensuring that the development of your strengths contributes meaningfully to your desired life outcomes.

5. **Regular Self-Assessment:**

   **Description:** Schedule regular self-assessment sessions to evaluate your progress. Reflect on how your strengths have been applied in different situations and their impact.

   **Application:** Regular assessment allows for course correction, adjustments to your plan, and a deeper understanding of how your strengths contribute to your growth and success.

6. **Feedback and Learning Loops:**

    **Description:** Seek feedback from others and create learning loops within your plan. Understand how your strengths are perceived by those around you and use insights to refine your approach.

    **Application:** Feedback and learning loops foster continuous improvement, ensuring your plan remains adaptable and responsive to evolving circumstances.

7. **Adaptability and Flexibility:**

    **Description:** Build adaptability and flexibility into your strength-based plan. Acknowledge that goals and circumstances may change and be prepared to adjust your plan accordingly.

    **Application:** An adaptable plan allows for resilience and ensures you can navigate unforeseen challenges without losing sight of your strengths-based objectives.

By incorporating these elements into your strength-based planning, you create a dynamic and comprehensive framework that capitalizes on your innate abilities and fosters continuous growth and achievement aligned with your unique strengths. Incorporating these elements into strength-based planning not only maximizes your potential but also enhances your sense of purpose and fulfillment. It enables you to navigate challenges with confidence, adaptability, and a clear sense of direction, ultimately leading to sustained personal and professional growth.

**Overcoming Challenges and Obstacles** - Overcoming challenges and obstacles involves resilience, adaptability, and strategic problem-solving, fostering personal growth and transforming setbacks into opportunities for learning and advancement.

1. **Navigating Challenges:** Cultivating strengths and talents does not exempt you from facing challenges. A Strengths-based approach, however, equips you with the resilience and adaptability needed to steer you through difficulties with a positive mindset. Navigating challenges is an inevitable part of any personal journey. However, adopting a strengths-based approach transforms how you face and overcome troubles. Instead of viewing challenges as insurmountable obstacles, cultivating strengths endows you with the resilience and adaptability needed to manage them with confidence.

2. **Seeking Support:** Seeking support is a crucial aspect of navigating challenges with a strengths-based approach. Collaboration with mentors, coaches, or peers who complement your strengths creates a synergistic environment for personal growth. These individuals can offer guidance, share experiences, and provide insights contributing to your ability to overcome challenges effectively.

The support network becomes a valuable resource, reinforcing your strengths and helping you cross the complexities of your journey with confidence and resilience.

When faced with challenges, a strengths-based mindset encourages you to draw upon your innate abilities, leveraging your natural talents to find innovative solutions and persevere through adversity. This approach doesn't eliminate obstacles but transforms them into opportunities for growth and learning. These elements form a powerful combination, ensuring that challenges become stepping stones rather than roadblocks on your path to personal and professional fulfillment.

**The Ripple Effect of Unveiling Potential** - Unveiling your potential creates a ripple effect, impacting personal growth, inspiring others, and contributing to a positive, transformative influence in both your life and the broader community.

1. **Personal Fulfillment:** Unveiling your potential can lead to a profound sense of personal fulfillment. Aligning with your innate strengths and talents provides an opportunity for you to experience a deep connection with your authentic self. Discovering and cultivating your potential through unveiling innate strengths and talents is a transformative journey that leads to profound personal fulfillment. When you align with your authentic self, a sense

of harmony and purpose permeates every aspect of your life. This connection with your true nature provides a solid foundation for personal growth and self-discovery, fostering a holistic sense of fulfillment beyond external achievements.

2. **Impact on Others:** Cultivating strengths and talents extends beyond personal satisfaction to positively impact those around you. Your authentic contributions inspire others to explore and unleash their own potential, creating a ripple effect in your community. As you authentically engage with your strengths, your actions and influences become a source of inspiration for those around you. This positive ripple effect creates a supportive and empowered community where individuals are encouraged to embrace their uniqueness and contribute their strengths to the collective journey. In essence, the journey toward personal fulfillment becomes a shared exploration, enriching your life and the lives of those you touch along the way.

### A Lifelong Journey of Unveiling

In painting the canvas of your life, unveiling your potential is a dynamic and continuous journey. 'Unveiling Your Potential" invites you to embark on this expedition with curiosity, self-awareness, and a commitment to growth. As you cultivate your strengths and nurture your talents, may you discover the depths of your capabilities and the unique contributions you bring forth to others.

In each unveiling, you add brushstrokes to the canvas of your existence, creating a masterpiece of authenticity, purpose, and fulfillment. May the exploration of your potential be a lifelong adventure, revealing new layers of strength, talent, and possibility with every step you take.

# CHAPTER 8

## "Dancing in the Rain - Finding Joy in Adversity"

### Illuminating Shadows: Overcoming Obstacles and Embracing Change

Life is a dance, and sometimes, it's amid storms. This chapter explores the transformative art of finding joy despite the adversities that inevitably come our way. Just as a skilled dancer moves gracefully through the raindrops, cultivating joy in challenging times is a profound and empowering expression of resilience and positivity.

**The Nature of Adversity** - Adversity is an inherent aspect of life, a dynamic force that confronts and shapes you, fostering resilience, growth, and transformative experiences. Embracing adversity as a catalyst for self-discovery empowers you to harness your inner strength, adaptability, and wisdom, ultimately leading to profound personal evolution and enlightenment.

1. **Understanding Adversity:** Adversity encompasses challenges, setbacks, and unexpected turns that test your resilience. Understanding adversity as an inherent aspect of the human journey is an essential paradigm shift that lays the foundation for resilience and joy. Instead of viewing challenges as anomalies to shy away from, acknowledging their inevitability allows you to approach life with a more realistic and empowered perspective. In its various forms, adversity becomes not only an expected companion but a potential catalyst for growth and transformation.

2. **The Power of Perception:** The way you perceive and interpret a situation greatly influences how you deal with adversity. It changes your perspective to view difficulties as chances for learning and progress rather than as insurmountable barriers, which makes it possible to find joy even in the most trying situations. By viewing obstacles as chances for development and education, you give yourself the power to derive significance and benefit from them. With this mental adjustment, adversity ceases to be a cause of discomfort and

instead becomes a blank canvas on which you can boldly illustrate your resiliency and fortitude.

As you navigate the twists and turns of life with a new perspective, the once daunting hurdles become stepping stones, and joy becomes a beacon that guides you through the storm. With understanding adversity and the intentional shaping of your perception, you unlock the profound capacity to find joy amidst life's inevitable challenges.

**Cultivating a Joyful Mindset** - Cultivating a joyful mindset involves consciously choosing positivity, finding gratitude in daily moments, and embracing an optimistic perspective to enhance overall well-being. Nurturing a joyful mindset entails cherishing simple pleasures, maintaining an open heart to life's beauty, and channeling resilience in the face of challenges, crafting a resilient and vibrant inner landscape.

1. **Choosing Joy:** Joy is a decision you make about how you handle the obstacles in your life as well as an outcome of the external environment. You can develop a joyful mentality by deliberately concentrating on the good events that have happened to you. Selecting joy is a life-changing choice that gives you the ability to face challenges head-on with optimism and perseverance. In this sense, joy becomes a state of mind that transcends outside conditions. It becomes a result of your deliberate decision to emphasize the positive

aspects of your experiences rather than being exclusively dependent on fortunate circumstances.

2. **Gratitude as a Gateway to Joy:** There are often aspects of your life for which you are thankful, even during trying times. Gratitude changes your viewpoint and enables you to find the bright side of hardship. It is a strong doorway to happiness and by embracing gratitude, it asks you to change your viewpoint and search within for the good even in the face of hardship. It invites you to recognize no matter how tiny, you have a cause for thankfulness. This change in perspective has a significant positive effect on your mental health by focusing your attention on the abundance in your life rather than what might be lacking.

3. **Embracing an Optimistic Perspective:** Taking a positive stance on life's obstacles is a transforming strategy. When you view challenges as chances for emotional and personal development, you develop a positive mindset. This resilient and determined way of thinking gives you the ability to face challenges head-on. When you have faith in your ability to overcome obstacles, you approach problems with an open mind and a willingness to uncover your hidden abilities. This perspective change entails more than just thinking positively; it also entails appreciating the positive aspects of every circumstance and cultivating a resilient

attitude that views setbacks as opportunities for growth and a more satisfying existence.

You can create a resilient foundation for navigating life's complexities by choosing joy and incorporating gratitude into your mindset. This intentional approach enhances your ability to find joy amidst challenges and fosters a sense of contentment and fulfillment that goes beyond external circumstances. In the tapestry of your experiences, the threads of joy and gratitude weave together to create a vibrant and resilient narrative.

**Embracing Resilience as a Source of Joy** – Resilience can be a profound source of joy. It involves finding strength in adversity, cultivating gratitude, and appreciating the transformative journey of personal growth. Empathy is developed through shared experiences, obstacles are overcome with grace, and doors to deep happiness and fulfillment are opened through developing resilience.

1. **Resilience in Action:** Resilience is not only about bouncing back from adversity but also about finding strength and joy in the process. Embracing challenges with a resilient mindset transforms difficulties into stepping stones for personal growth. When put into action, resilience is about discovering strength and joy amid the challenges. Within the process of navigating through

challenges, resilience truly shines, enabling you to endure and thrive despite your adversities.

2. **Learning from Adversity:** Adversity provides profound lessons and a deepened sense of joy comes from extracting wisdom from them. Difficulties and challenges, often seen as an opposing force, becomes an influential teacher when approached with the right mindset. The saying "we learn best when we fail" encapsulates that challenges and setbacks can be rich sources of wisdom. Instead of viewing adversity as a setback, rethink it as an avenue to learn, adapt, and grow, which fosters a more profound sense of happiness. Joy, then, arises from overcoming difficulties and the wisdom gained in the process.

In essence, resilience in action involves a dynamic engagement with life's challenges, where each hurdle becomes a platform for learning, adaptation, and personal triumph. The joy in this process is not just a fleeting emotion but a lasting sense of fulfillment that stems from the continuous journey of growth and self-discovery.

**The Freedom of Acceptance** - The freedom of acceptance liberates the mind, fostering peace by embracing life as it unfolds, unburdened by the need for control or resistance. The power of surrender is unleashed through acceptance, which enables you to dance to the beat of life, accepting each moment with grace and composure and promoting a deep sense of inner peace and tranquility.

1. **Acceptance of What Is:** Finding joy in adversity often begins with accepting the present reality. While it doesn't mean resignation, acceptance allows you to direct your energies toward constructive responses rather than futile resistance. The journey to find joy in adversity is intricately tied to the principles of acceptance and letting go. It is a conscious decision to confront the truth of the situation, recognizing that some aspects of life are beyond your control. In doing so, you free yourself from the energy-draining refusal to accept to circumstances you cannot change. Acceptance becomes a gateway to redirect your focus and energy towards responses that are constructive, empowering, and aligned with your well-being.

2. **Freedom in Letting Go:** Letting go of the need to control and surrendering to the ebb and flow of life is liberating. The freedom found in letting go opens an avenue for joy to emerge. In tandem with acceptance, the concept of freedom in letting go adds another layer to the pursuit of joy. It involves relinquishing the need for excessive control and surrendering to life's natural waves. This act releases you from the burdens of trying to manipulate outcomes beyond your influence. In the space created by letting go, a profound sense of

freedom surfaces, even in the face of challenges. It is a recognition that, despite external circumstances, you possess the internal freedom to choose your responses, fostering a resilient and joyful mindset that transcends the limitations of uncontrollable events.

3. And creates a space for happiness. The idea of freedom in letting go, when combined with acceptance, provides another level to the search for happiness. It entails letting go of the demand for excessive control and allowing life to flow naturally. By doing this, you relieve yourself of the pressure of attempting to control events that are outside of your control. Even in the face of difficulties, a deep sense of liberation emerges in the space made possible by letting go. It is an understanding that you have the internal freedom to choose your reactions regardless of the external conditions, which cultivates a resilient and joyous attitude that transcends the restrictions.

**Joyful Practices in Daily Life** - Joyful practices in daily life involve fostering gratitude, savoring moments, and fostering connections, creating a tapestry of positivity woven into each day. Incorporating mindful reflection, embracing kindness, and cultivating empathy enriches our experiences, weaving threads of fulfillment and contentment into the fabric of your daily life.

1. **Mindful Presence:** Mindful presence and cultivating hobbies are potent avenues for infusing joy into your life, especially during challenging times. Adopting practices, such as meditation, deep breathing, or simply savoring the present moment, allows you to connect with the richness of your immediate surroundings. Being fully present fosters a heightened awareness of the beauty and positivity within the here and now. This mindfulness becomes a source of joy as it redirects your attention from the uncertainties of the future or the challenges of the past to the simple yet profound pleasures of the present.

2. **Cultivating Hobbies:** Fostering hobbies and dedicating time to activities that bring genuine joy is another key to enhancing your overall well-being. Hobbies and creative pursuits serve as outlets for self-expression and personal enjoyment. Whether it's painting, writing, playing a musical instrument, or any other passion, these undertakings provide a means of escape, a sanctuary where you can immerse yourself in the activities that bring you happiness. The sense of accomplishment and fulfillment derived from dedicating time to these pursuits contributes significantly to your emotional resilience, acting as a buffer against adversities.

Even in the face of difficulties, engaging in hobbies and maintaining a conscious presence serve as the harmonizing notes that make up a melody of delight in life. While hobbies provide opportunities for self-expression and pleasure, they also provide a delightful change that may be uplifted even in the face of obstacles and mindful presence cultivates an awareness of the existing moment.

**Finding Joy in Small Moments** – Finding joy in small moments means appreciating the simplicity of life, acknowledging the beauty in everyday occurrences, and savoring those fleeting yet precious instances.

1. **Small but Joyful Moments:** Joy doesn't always come in grand gestures. More often than not, it resides in the small everyday moments. Nurturing an awareness of these moments is a practice that can profoundly impact your well-being. Whether it's the warmth of sunlight on a chilly morning, the sound of laughter echoing through the air, the comfort of a warm cup of tea, or the refreshing coolness of a beverage on a hot day, these seemingly small experiences hold immense potential for joy. By consciously savoring and appreciating these moments as they come, you open yourself to the beauty inherent in the ordinary, transforming routine into a series of delightful experiences.

2. **Gratitude Journaling:** Create a gratitude journal to document moments of joy and appreciation. Gratitude journaling serves as a powerful companion on this journey. It provides a dedicated

space to document and reflect on moments of joy and appreciation. Regularly revisiting these entries amplifies the positive aspects of your life, contributing to the development of a joy-filled mindset. It becomes a tangible record of the richness of your experiences, acting as a source of inspiration during challenging times.

In essence, recognizing small moments of joy and the act of gratitude journaling serve as intentional pathways to infuse your life with joy, proving that happiness often resides in the small but significant moments that color your everyday existence.

**Creativity as a Joyful Outlet** - Creativity as a joyful outlet allows self-expression, exploration, and the liberation of imagination, fostering a sense of accomplishment, fulfillment, and happiness.

1. **Expressive Arts:** Engage in expressive arts as a means of processing emotions and finding joy. Participating in arts, such as painting, writing, music, or dance, provides a cathartic and joyful outlet for processing emotions and allows you to delve into the depths of your feelings, transforming complex emotions into tangible expressions of art. The intentional act of creation becomes a source of joy, offering a sense of accomplishment and liberation as your inner world finds external

manifestation. Expressive arts provide joy in the process and offer a tangible creation that you can revisit, serving as a testament to your emotional journey.

**Mindful Movement:** Incorporate mindful movement practices into your routine. Activities like yoga, tai chi, or simply going for a mindful walk connect body and mind, fostering a sense of joy through movement. Mindful movement practices intertwine the body and mind in a harmonious dance. These activities cultivate a heightened awareness of your body and the surrounding environment, fostering a sense of joy through movement. Mindful movement encourages you to be fully present, appreciating each movement's sensations, rhythms, and nuances.

Expressive arts and mindful movement are powerful gateways to joy, offering unique avenues for self-expression, emotional release, and a deeper connection with the present moment. The joy derived from such practices lies in the unity of mind and body, creating a holistic experience that contributes to overall well-being. Through the practice of expressive arts and mindful movement, you take a transforming journey that strengthens your inner connection to yourself and the present moment, increasing your joy.

**Joy in Connection and Relationships** - Joy in connection and relationships emerges from shared experiences, emotional support, and genuine connections, creating a sense of belonging and shared happiness.

1. **Nurturing Connections:** Joy is often amplified in the company of others. In the tapestry of joy, the threads of meaningful connections and acts of kindness weave a vibrant pattern that extends beyond individual experiences. Nurturing connections with friends and family adds depth to life's joy. Shared experiences, laughter, and the warmth of companionship create moments that resonate with lasting happiness. The support and understanding found in meaningful relationships become a source of strength, enhancing a sense of joy in your life.

2. **Acts of Kindness:** Engage in acts of kindness for others. Contributing to the well-being of others creates a sense of purpose and joy. Acts of kindness, whether grand or modest, are like seeds of joy planted in the collective garden of humanity. Engaging in these activities on behalf of others can contribute to their well-being and generate a profound sense of purpose and happiness within you. The beauty lies in their ripple effect—they can create a positive impact not only on the recipient but also on you as the giver as well as those who bear witness or might be inspired by these gestures.

By fostering connections and embracing acts of kindness, you contribute to a shared reservoir of joy that uplifts your personal growth, including that of the wider community, creating a harmonious symphony of happiness reverberating far beyond your individual moments.

**Resilience in the Face of Major Adversity** - Being resilient in the face of severe hardship requires inner strength, flexibility, and a steadfast dedication to facing obstacles head-on with bravery and determination.

1. **Major Loss and Grief:** Finding joy in the face of major adversity, such as loss or grief, is a profound journey. Navigating significant loss and grief can be arduous, and finding joy amidst profound adversity requires a delicate balance between honoring emotions and seeking solace. In the face of significant losses, it is normal to experience a spectrum of emotions, from intense sorrow to moments of numbness. Acknowledging and processing these emotions is an important step in the healing process.

   Seeking support becomes a cornerstone in the pursuit of joy amidst grief. Whether through friends, family, or professional counseling, having a network of understanding individuals fosters a space where emotions can be expressed without judgment. The shared burden of grief often lightens when carried together.

2. **Post-Traumatic Growth:** Post-traumatic growth is the phenomenon (first developed by Richard Tedeschi, Ph.D. and Lawrence Calhoun, Ph.D. 1996) where individuals emerge from adversity with a heightened sense of purpose and joy. Embracing the potential for growth and positive transformation in the aftermath of significant challenges is a testament to resilience. It is an acknowledgment that you can emerge with a heightened sense of purpose and joy even after facing profound challenges.

   Post-traumatic growth represents the remarkable resilience of the human spirit. This process involves coping with adversity and actively seeking meaning and positive transformation. It reflects your innate ability to find strength within yourself, turning the darkness of loss into a canvas for growth, resilience, and, ultimately, joy. Embracing the potential for post-traumatic growth is a testament to the human capacity for resilience and the unwavering pursuit of joy, even in the face of life's most challenging chapters.

**The Joyful Mindset as a Lifelong Practice** – A joyful mindset is a way of living that includes developing optimism, finding joy in the small things in life, and accepting resilience as an ongoing process of development and appreciation.

1. **Continual Growth:** Developing and refining a joyful mindset is an ongoing process. In cultivating a joyful mindset, continual growth is akin to tending to a garden—requiring consistent care, attention, and a genuine curiosity for the evolving landscape of your inner world. The journey toward joy is not a static path but a dynamic process of self-discovery and adaptation to life's ever-changing circumstances. It calls for an open-minded approach, allowing you to learn from your experiences, adjust your perspectives, and discover new sources of joy along the way. Embrace the journey with a spirit of curiosity and openness.

2. **Integration with Other Principles:** The principles explored in earlier chapters, such as resilience, positivity, and strength development, work together to pursue joy. Moreover, integrating principles explored in these chapters is fundamental to the holistic pursuit of happiness.

    A. Resilience equips you to navigate challenges on this journey, turning them into opportunities for growth.

    B. Positivity acts as a guiding light, illuminating joyful moments even in adversity.

    C. Strength development empowers you to leverage our innate capabilities, creating a more fulfilling and meaningful existence.

The seamless integration of these principles forms a robust framework that sustains and enhances your ability to lead a joy-filled life. By weaving these threads together, you create a tapestry of well-being, resilience, and purpose, where joy becomes an intrinsic part of your ongoing personal growth and fulfillment journey.

### Dancing Into the Future

As you embark on the dance of life, may you find joy in every step, even when faced with the unexpected rhythms of adversity. "Dancing in the Rain" invites you to embrace the transformative power of joy, to revel in the small moments, and to dance with resilience through the storms.

In your dance, may joy become the melody that guides your steps, the rhythm that sustains your spirit, and the energy that propels you forward. May you discover that even amidst the raindrops, there is a dance waiting to be danced, and within that dance, a joy exists that transcends the challenges of the moment.

# CHAPTER 9

# "Connecting with Others: Building Supportive Relationships"

## Harvesting Happiness: Cultivating Joy in Daily Life

In the journey towards personal fulfillment, the road to meaningful relationships winds a path that adds warmth, support, and richness to our lives. This chapter explores the profound impact of building and nurturing supportive relationships. Just as a tree draws strength from its roots, cultivating connections with others provides a foundation for growth, resilience, and a fulfilling life.

**The Significance of Relationships** - Relationships are the threads weaving the fabric of your life, offering support, connection, and shared experiences that enrich your journey with meaning and depth. They serve as mirrors reflecting our joys, sorrows, and growth, fostering a sense of belonging and purpose that transcends individual experience, enriching the human connection.

1. **Foundation for Well-Being:** Relationships form the cornerstone of our emotional well-being. They create a tapestry that represents the depth of your emotional landscape. When you establish and maintain meaningful relationships, you impact your sense of purpose, belonging, and general happiness in life. The quality of your connections frequently turns into a poignant mirror reflecting the quality of your existence in the complex dance of human interaction.

2. **Impact on Mental Health:** Having supportive social networks is linked to better mental health. Good relationships ease stress, foster a sense of stability, offer emotional support, and can become a vital source of stability during trying circumstances. Strong social ties serve as a protective barrier against life's obstacles. The offered emotional support then turns into a crucial tool for overcoming tension, hardship, and uncertainty. Supportive relationships are mutually beneficial because they create a space

where you can express your happiness and sadness, which enhances overall wellbeing beyond personal experiences.

The interplay of interpersonal relationships, emotional well-being, and mental health highlights the intricate and profound impact that connections with others have on the quality of our lives. Interpersonal relationships form the tapestry of your emotional well-being and mental health, influencing the depth and richness of your life. The profound impact of meaningful connections resonates in the quality of your overall well-being.

**Understanding Relationship Dynamics** - Understanding relationship dynamics involves navigating the intricate interplay of communication, mutual support, and shared growth, fostering connections that contribute positively to individual and collective well-being.

1. **Types of Relationships:** Relationships come in various forms, including family, friendships, romantic partners, and professional connections. Each type plays a unique role in your life, fulfilling different emotional and social needs. Relationships form a diverse and dynamic tapestry in the fabric of your life, each type contributing unique threads that weave together to create a rich and nuanced picture.

A. Family relationships provide a foundation of love and belonging, grounding you in a shared history and heritage.

B. Friendships offer companionship, shared experiences, and the joy of mutual understanding.

C. Romantic partnerships deepen emotional intimacy and provide a space for vulnerability and romantic love.

D. Professional connections contribute to your growth and development, offering opportunities for collaboration, mentorship, and career advancement.

2. **Reciprocity and Trust:** Healthy relationships are built and thrive on reciprocity and trust. The essence of reciprocity lies in the give-and-take dynamic, where one contributes to the relationship's growth and well-being. This reciprocity fosters a sense of balance, ensuring both parties feel valued and supported. Like a delicate but resilient bridge, trust connects us, allowing each to share their vulnerabilities, dreams, and challenges. Trust is the unseen thread that binds relationships, enabling them to deepen, flourish, and withstand the tests of time.

In embracing the diversity of relationships and nurturing reciprocity and trust, you cultivate a social terrain that enriches your emotional and social well-being. Recognizing and valuing the distinct roles that different relationships play in your life contributes to a holistic and interconnected experience of your well-being.

**The Art of Communication** - The art of communication involves the skillful exchange of thoughts and emotions, promoting understanding, connection, and the cultivation of healthy relationships. Effective communication serves as a bridge, fostering empathy and mutual respect, nurturing an environment where voices are heard and perspectives are valued, strengthening the bonds that unite individuals in harmony.

1. **Effective Communication:** Communication is the lifeblood of relationships. Developing and honing practical communication skills involves active listening, expressing yourself clearly, and fostering an open and honest dialogue. A candid conversation, clear expression of yourself, and active listening are all necessary for acquiring and improving practical communication skills. Understanding and connection pulse with the rhythm of effective communication. It entails using clear language and practicing active listening, which goes beyond simply hearing what is being said to actually comprehend the feelings, viewpoints, and intentions that are being conveyed.

Clear communication is the conductor in the symphony of relationships, arranging harmony and coherence.

2. **Empathy and Compassion:** Empathy is defined as the ability to understand and share the feelings of others, and compassion is a genuine concern for others' well-being. These are essential elements in meaningful connections and cultivating these qualities deepens the emotional bond in relationships. It is the ability to walk in someone else's shoes and share their feelings, creating bridges of understanding. Empathy fosters a sense of being heard and acknowledged, forming a basis for genuine connection, while compassion acts as a nurturing force, enveloping relationships in warmth and support. Empathy and compassion infuse relationships with a depth of emotional resonance, transforming them from mere interactions into meaningful connections.

Relationships blossom into vibrant expressions of shared understanding and mutual care in the intricate dance of effective communication, empathy, and compassion. When cultivated and practiced, these qualities create a relational landscape where you can feel seen, heard, and valued—a fertile ground for the seeds of connection to flourish and thrive.

**Building and Maintaining Friendships** - Building and maintaining friendships requires authenticity, empathy, and mutual support, fostering connections that enrich your life with shared experiences and genuine companionship. Friendships thrive on reciprocity, evolving through shared laughter, tears, and growth. They provide solace in times of need, celebrate victories, and form an irreplaceable foundation of trust and understanding.

1. **Initiating Friendships:** Stepping outside of your comfort zone and keeping an open mind are necessary for forming new acquaintances. Creating friendships is an exciting and brave act that immerses you in the complex web of human connection. From there, you can go out on a quest to find common ground within the plethora of social opportunities. Like-minded people are drawn into your orbit by shared interests, hobbies, or values, which work as magnetic forces. It's a dance of openness and vulnerability, hearts being unlocked to the possibility of new connections.

2. **Nurturing Friendships:** Friendships requires effort and attention. Regular communication, mutual support, and spending quality time together contribute to the longevity and depth of the relationship. Like a delicate plant, friendships require dedicated care and attention to thrive.

    A. Regular communication becomes the lifeblood that sustains the connection. Sharing ideas, emotions, and experiences is equally as important as verbal communication. It's the bridge that spans the gaps and keeps the connection alive.

B. Mutual support is the pillar that upholds the structure of friendship. It's the assurance that there is someone to lean on or share the triumphs in times of challenge or joy. The strength of these bonds is often tested and refined through the storms of life, solidifying the trust and understanding between friends.

C. Spending quality time together is the sunlight that nourishes the friendship. Whether engaging in shared activities, deep conversations, or simple moments of joy, these experiences add depth and color to the relational canvas. It's an investment that pays rich dividends through a resilient, enduring connection.

Initiating and nurturing friendships is a symphony of intentionality, care, and reciprocity. It's a testament to the richness that unfolds when individuals come together, sharing the common ground and the journey of growth and mutual support.

**Family Dynamics and Support** - Family dynamics and support form the foundation of your life, shaping your identity and providing a sense of belonging, love, and security. Within the embrace of family, you find sanctuary amidst life's storms, sharing in traditions, memories, and unconditional love that nurture your spirits and anchor you in a world of constant change.

1. **Family Bonds:** Whether biological or chosen, family bonds form the bedrock of your emotional landscape, providing you with a sense of belonging and continuity. Establishing and nurturing these bonds entails a delicate dance of understanding, acceptance, and a steadfast commitment to each other's well-being. The strength of family bonds lies not in their absence of challenges but in the collective ability to navigate them. Effective communication then becomes the linchpin, allowing family members to express their thoughts, concerns, and emotions openly.

2. **Navigating Family Challenges:** Families are complicated and may face challenges, conflicts, and transitions. Effective communication, empathy, and a shared commitment to resolution contribute to navigating these challenges and maintaining family support. A shared commitment to resolution is the compass that guides families through turbulent times. It involves a collective decision to address challenges proactively, seeking solutions that prioritize the well-being of the family unit. This commitment is a testament to the enduring strength of family bonds.

In short, family bonds are a dynamic and evolving journey. They require constant attention, communication, and a willingness to adapt to the changing landscapes of individual growth and shared experiences. By cultivating understanding, embracing empathy, and fostering a commitment to resolution, families can weave a resilient tapestry that stands the test of time.

**Romantic Relationships and Intimacy** - Romantic relationships and intimacy bring depth, connection, and emotional fulfillment, enriching life with shared experiences, mutual support, and a profound sense of companionship. Souls entwine within love relationships, creating a tapestry of passion and comprehension. Partners navigate life's path together through vulnerability and affection, finding comfort and ecstasy in each other's embrace.

1. **Building Intimacy:** Intimate relationships involve a deep emotional connection, vulnerability, and shared experiences. Building intimacy requires trust, open communication, and a willingness to be authentic with one another.

    A. Building intimacy in relationships is akin to constructing a bridge of emotional connection that requires a sturdy foundation of trust, open communication, and a commitment to authenticity. Intimate relationships thrive on vulnerability, the willingness to share your deepest thoughts, fears, and aspirations.

Trust acts as the bedrock of this emotional connection, creating a safe space to reveal your true self without fear of judgment.

B. Open communication is the mortar that binds the stones of intimacy together. Honest and transparent dialogue fosters understanding, deepening the emotional connection between partners. It involves sharing the positive aspects of your life and addressing concerns, conflicts, and insecurities constructively.

C. Authenticity is the essence of intimacy. It involves being genuine to yourself within the relationship. Embracing vulnerability and authenticity invites a reciprocal response, creating a dynamic where both partners can grow individually and together.

2. **Sustaining Romance:** Romantic relationships involve ongoing effort and investment. Shared goals, mutual values, and maintaining a sense of novelty contribute to the relationship's longevity and vibrancy with a joint vision of the future which adds depth and meaning to the romantic connection. Maintaining a sense of novelty is the spice that keeps the flame of romance alive. While routine is a part of every relationship, introducing new experiences, surprises, and shared adventures injects freshness and excitement. The exploration of new facets of the relationship rejuvenates the

romantic connection, ensuring that it evolves and deepens over time.

In essence, building intimacy and sustaining romance are reciprocal endeavors. They involve mutual commitment, communication, and a shared investment in the growth and well-being of the relationship. As the couple weaves the threads of trust, communication, authenticity, shared goals, and novelty, they create a tapestry of enduring and vibrant love.

**Professional/Trade Networks and Mentoring -** Professional or trade networks and mentoring are invaluable assets in career or entrepreneurial development. These associations provide avenues for expanding connections, accessing opportunities, and exchanging knowledge. Mentoring offers guidance, support, and wisdom from experienced individuals, aiding in skill development, career or trade progression, and personal growth. Together, they foster a dynamic ecosystem where expertise is shared, relationships are cultivated, and success is nurtured through collaboration and teaching.

1. **Building Professional Connections:** Professional relationships are valuable for career growth and personal development. Building a professional network involves effective communication, collaboration, and a willingness to support and learn from colleagues.

Developing a network of professional contacts is essential to both personal and professional growth. Successful relationships in the ever-changing professional or trade worlds are based on effective communication and collaboration. It involves active listening, understanding unique perspectives, and fostering an environment of mutual respect.

A. Collaboration, both within and outside your immediate work team, can lead to innovative solutions and the exchange of valuable insights.

B. A willingness to support and learn from colleagues is essential for the reciprocal nature of professional relationships. By offering assistance when needed and being open to receiving guidance, individuals contribute to the collective growth of the professional community.

2. **Mentorship and Guidance:** Mentoring relationships offer direction and assistance in overcoming obstacles in both the personal and professional spheres. Building a mutually beneficial relationship is advantageous for both mentors and mentees. Professional relationships greatly benefit from mentoring, which provides direction and encouragement to individuals pursuing career choices.

Relationships between mentors and mentees flourish when ideas, viewpoints, and experiences are shared. Mentees bring energy and new viewpoints, and mentors offer insightful guidance. Building professional connections is not just about expanding your network; it's about cultivating meaningful and mutually beneficial relationships. Through effective communication, collaboration, and mentorship, you can navigate the intricacies of your career, gain valuable insight, and contribute to the growth of the broader professional community.

**The Role of Boundaries** - Establishing clear boundaries fosters healthy relationships by defining limits, preserving individual autonomy, and creating a framework for mutual respect, understanding, and emotional well-being.

Setting healthy boundaries is crucial for cultivating thriving relationships. It involves a delicate dance of communicating your needs while respecting the needs of others. This mutual understanding builds trust and ensures that you feel heard and valued within the relationship.

1. **Setting Healthy Boundaries:** Well-defined boundaries are the cornerstone of healthy relationships. Setting boundaries involves:

    A. **Communicating your needs:** Communication plays a pivotal role o boundary-setting. Expressing your needs, desires, and limitations fosters clarity and prevents misunderstandings. Open and honest communication creates a foundation for understanding, reinforcing interpersonal connections, and establishing a harmonious balance in relationships.

B. **Respecting the needs of others:** Additionally, being receptive to the needs communicated by others promotes empathy and strengthens the overall fabric of the relationship. Respecting the needs of others is a reciprocal act of empathy. By acknowledging and honoring the communicated needs of those around you, relationships flourish with mutual understanding and a harmonious exchange of respect.

C. **Establishing a balance between connection and autonomy:** Setting limits requires a subtle art in striking a balance between liberty and connection. It means finding a middle ground where you maintain your independence and personal space while actively participating in the shared aspects of the relationship. This equilibrium ensures that both parties feel safe and supported, contributing to the overall health and sustainability of the connection.

2. **Respecting Individuality:** Recognizing and respecting each person's individuality in a

relationship is vital to sustainability. Allowing space for personal growth, pursuits, and self-discovery contributes to the health and longevity of connections. Acknowledging and celebrating each person's uniqueness fosters an environment where personal growth, pursuits, and self-discovery are supported and encouraged. Embracing each person's individuality adds depth to the connection, allowing the relationship to evolve while providing the space for both partners to flourish.

In essence, setting healthy boundaries and respecting individuality in relationships is a dynamic process that requires ongoing communication, understanding, and a commitment to fostering an environment where both autonomy and connection thrive.

**Overcoming Relationship Challenges** - Overcoming relationship challenges demands a delicate balance of patience, empathy, and communication. It involves a journey of understanding, where both parties navigate through differences with mutual respect and a willingness to compromise. It's about embracing vulnerability, acknowledging flaws, and working together to build trust and resilience. Through adversity, relationships can emerge stronger, forged by the fires of shared experiences and a commitment to growth and connection.

1. **Communication During Conflict:** Conflict is a natural part of relationships. Effective communication during conflict is an art that can significantly impact the health and resilience of a relationship. It requires a combination of active listening, constructive expression of emotions, and a collaborative approach to finding resolutions.

2. **Active listening** - involves hearing not just the spoken words, but genuinely understanding the underlying emotions and perspectives. Creating an environment where both parties feel supported and validated is essential during conflict. Often, this involves paraphrasing, summarizing, and acknowledging the emotions expressed by the other person.

3. **Constructively expressing emotions** - is another crucial aspect. Instead of placing blame or becoming defensive, you can share your feelings using "I" statements, expressing your emotions without attacking the other person. This approach fosters a more open and non-confrontational atmosphere conducive to resolving the conflict.

4. **Counseling and Support:** In times of significant relationship challenges, seeking professional counseling can provide valuable insights and strategies. Professional support offers a neutral space for communication and problem-solving. They bring expertise in facilitating constructive dialogue, helping each person understand the

other's perspectives, and guiding them toward healthier ways of interacting. Counseling can address current conflicts and equip you with tools and strategies for effective communication, conflict resolution, and long-term relationship growth. It can be a proactive and empowering step to strengthen the foundations of a relationship, promoting understanding, empathy, and resilience in the face of challenges.

**Friendships Across Generations** - Friendships across generations enrich life with diverse perspectives and shared wisdom, fostering mutual growth and creating lasting connections that transcend age-related boundaries.

1. **Inter-Generational Connections:** Building connections across generations enhances our understanding of different perspectives and experiences. Friendships with people of various ages contribute to a rich tapestry of insights and support. Inter-generational connections offer a unique and enriching dimension to your social fabric by fostering friendships across various age groups. Building relationships with individuals from different generations offers a diverse perspectives, experiences, and cultural backgrounds.

2. **Mutual Learning:** Friendships with people from different generations provide opportunities for mutual learning. Shared experiences, wisdom,

and cultural insights enrich the lives of both parties. Each generation brings its own set of experiences, wisdom, and cultural insights to the table. Sharing stories, traditions, and life lessons becomes a two-way street where both parties stand to gain valuable insights. Younger individuals can learn from the wisdom and experiences of their older counterparts, while older individuals may find inspiration and fresh perspectives from the younger generation.

These connections can bridge generational gaps, dispel stereotypes, and foster a sense of unity and understanding. Embracing diversity in friendships across age groups promotes a more inclusive and interconnected society where individuals of all ages contribute to each other's personal growth and well-being. The interplay of shared experiences and diverse viewpoints in inter-generational connections contributes to a more vibrant social landscape.

**The Digital Landscape of Relationships** - Navigating the digital landscape of relationships involves mindful communication, fostering connections through technology, and balancing virtual interactions with meaningful face-to-face engagements for genuine connection.

1. **Social Media and Connections:** The digital age has transformed how we connect. Social media platforms provide opportunities for staying in touch,

sharing experiences, and building connections. It is essential, however, to balance online interactions with face-to-face contacts. In today's digitally-driven world, social media platforms are powerful tools for fostering ties, enabling you to transcend physical barriers and engage with people from diverse backgrounds and cultures. These programs offer instant communication, allowing you to impart your interests with a broader audience in real-time. However, amidst the convenience and accessibility of online interaction, it's imperative to recognize the importance of maintaining authentic connections through face-to-face encounters.

2. **Maintaining Authenticity:** Authenticity remains crucial in the digital landscape. Balancing the convenience of online communication with authentic, in-person interactions ensures genuine and meaningful connections. While social media facilitates communication and relationship-building, it can sometimes lead to superficial interactions or disconnection from reality. Authenticity in relationships is developed through genuine, heartfelt conversations, shared experiences, and meaningful gestures that can only be fully expressed in person. Face-to-face interactions allow for deeper connections, genuine empathy, and a better understanding of each other's nuances and emotions. Therefore, while leveraging the benefits of social media for connectivity and

networking, it's crucial to prioritize real-world interactions and experiences.

By balancing online communication and in-person engagement, we can nurture more authentic, fulfilling relationships and our personal growth. Balancing online communication and in-person engagement cultivates a holistic approach to relationships, fostering authenticity and personal growth. It allows for deeper connections through the seamless integration of virtual and real-world interactions.

**The Joy of Giving and Receiving -** The happiness that comes from giving and receiving is a mutual dance that strengthens bonds via moments of kindness and appreciation while fostering a peaceful flow of good energy. In the intertwined rhythm of this exchange, each act becomes a thread weaving through the fabric of relationships, enriching connections with the vibrant hues of empathy and understanding.

1. **Reciprocity in Relationships:** A healthy balance between giving and receiving is necessary in partnerships. The joy derived from contributing to others' well-being is as significant as accepting support when needed. In relationships, reciprocity is the dynamic interplay of support for one another, where the pleasure of giving and receiving fosters a cordial exchange. Healthy relationships depend on striking a balance between the satisfaction that comes from helping others and the gratitude that

comes from being supported when necessary. This harmony creates a strong foundation of mutual benefit and deep trust that supports long-lasting partnerships.

2. **Acts of Kindness:** Acts of kindness contribute to the joy within relationships. Being kind creates an environment that is upbeat and encouraging, fostering a sense of unity and shared humanity. Kindness, no matter how small or large, is the lifeblood of relationships. Small acts such as a nice message, a helpful hand, or a straightforward show of concern, can drastically change the dynamic of a relationship. It elevates the connection within the bond by fostering a good and encouraging atmosphere. It's a language that speaks louder than words, expressing a deep empathy and understanding that fortifies these bonds. Kindness creates a happy environment where people feel recognized, appreciated, and connected in the most genuine and meaningful ways.

### ▪ The Tapestry of Connection

As you navigate the intricate tapestry of your life, may the threads of meaningful connections weave a pattern of support, understanding, and joy. "Connecting with Others" invites you to embrace the transformative power of relationships, recognizing them as pillars that uphold the structure of your personal fulfillment.

In the dance of connection, may you find joy, comfort, and resilience. May the relationships you develop be a source of strength, a mirror reflecting your growth, and a celebration of the shared human experience. As you build and nurture connections, may your life be enriched by the tapestry of meaningful relationships that contribute to a fulfilling and purposeful existence.

# CHAPTER 10

## *"Living Your Spectrum: Creating a Fulfillment and Meaningful Life"*

### | Living Your Brilliance: Sustaining Positivity and Sharing Your Light

In the final chapter of this journey toward personal fulfillment, we explore "Living Your Spectrum." Life is a spectrum of experiences, emotions, and possibilities, and within this, you have the power to craft a fulfilling and meaningful life. This chapter serves as a culmination of the principles and practices discussed throughout the book, guiding you to create a life that reflects your values, passions, and unique identity.

**Understanding Your Spectrum** - Understanding your spectrum involves recognizing the nuances of your emotions, thoughts, and experiences, embracing the diversity within yourself, and navigating the complexities of your unique identity. It requires acknowledging the intricacies of your internal landscape, celebrating the multifaceted nature of your being, and embracing self-discovery.

1. **The Multifaceted Nature of Life:** Life unfolds in myriad ways, presenting a tapestry of experiences, challenges, and joys. Acknowledging the multifaceted nature of life allows you to embrace its diverse spectrum and appreciate its richness. Life is a kaleidoscope of experiences, each contributing to our existence's intricate pattern. From the highs of joy to the lows of challenge, the multifaceted nature of life weaves a tapestry that is uniquely yours.

2. **The Importance of Authenticity:** Living your spectrum begins with authenticity. Embracing authenticity is a key ingredient in crafting a genuine and meaningful life. Living authentically and intentionally aligns our choices, actions, and relationships with your true self. It's about peeling away layers of societal expectations or external influences to reveal the core of who you are. When you live authentically, you honor your individuality and contribute a genuine thread to the collective tapestry of the human experience.

Authenticity becomes the compass guiding you through life's twists and turns. It empowers you to make choices that resonate with your values and aspirations, fostering a sense of purpose and fulfillment. As you embrace the multifaceted nature of life with authenticity, you can unlock the door to a genuine and meaningful existence, where each color and shade adds depth and beauty to the canvas of your journey.

**Defining Fulfillment on Your Terms** - Defining fulfillment on your terms is a deeply personal journey, rooted in self-awareness and authenticity. It entails breaking free from societal expectations and external validations, and instead, honoring your unique values, passions, and aspirations. It's about embracing the freedom to craft a life that aligns with your deepest desires and brings a sense of purpose and joy. Fulfillment flourishes when you prioritize inner fulfillment over external measures of success, embracing what truly resonates with your soul.

1. **Clarifying Personal Values:** Reflect on your core values and beliefs. What principles guide your decisions and actions? Clarifying personal values is akin to setting the coordinates on the compass of your life. When you take the time to reflect on your fundamental beliefs and principles, you gain clarity on the direction you want to move. These values become the guiding stars that navigate you through life's myriad experiences. They are the unwavering standards that shape your decisions, actions, and relationships, ensuring that you stay

true to your authentic self amidst the curves and bends of life's spectrum.

2. **Identifying Personal Passions:** Passion is that fire in your belly that moves you forward. What are the activities, pursuits, or causes that ignite a sense of joy and purpose within you? Identifying personal passions is like discovering the fuel that propels you onward. Passion is the heartbeat of a fulfilling life, infusing your endeavors with enthusiasm and purpose. You unlock a reservoir of energy and joy when you recognize the activities, pursuits, or causes that spark that inner flame. Integrating these passions into your daily existence transforms the mundane into the extraordinary, adding depth and meaning to your journey.

Clarifying values and embracing passions create a harmonious choreography in the dance of life that enables you to travel across the spectrum with purpose and intention. It involves creating a life that is in tune with who you really are, one in which your passions drive every action and your values serve as a compass.

**Crafting a Personal Mission Statement** - Crafting a personal mission statement involves distilling your core values, aspirations, and principles into a succinct declaration that guides your decisions and actions with purpose and clarity.

1. **The Purpose of a Mission Statement:** Develop a personal mission statement that encompasses your values, passions, and overarching goals. A mission statement serves as a guiding beacon, offering coherence and a targeted approach to your life. It is akin to designing the blueprint of your life's purpose, and not just a collection of words; it's a living, breathing map that provides clarity, direction, and focus as you navigate the ever-changing terrain of life's landscape.

    Well-written personal mission statements usually consist of a few essential components that together express your values, interests, and main objectives.

    **Here are some essential components:**

    A. **Core Values:**
    - Describes the fundamental principles and beliefs that guide your decisions and actions.
    - Identifies the ethical and moral standards that are central to your character.

    B. **Passions and Interests:**
    - Highlights the activities, pursuits, or causes that ignite a sense of joy, purpose, and fulfillment within you.

- Reflects what you are genuinely enthusiastic about and what brings meaning to your life.

C. **Long-Term Goals and Aspirations:**

- Outlines your overarching objectives and the direction you aim to take in your life.
- Focuses on both personal and professional aspirations that align with your values.

D. **Contribution and Impact:**

- Expresses how you want to make a positive difference in the world or the lives of others.
- Articulates the impact you aspire to have through your actions and choices.

E. **Principles for Decision-Making:**

- Provides a set of guiding principles that influence your decision-making process.
- Helps you navigate choices that align with your mission and values.

F. **Reflection of Authentic Self:**

- Captures your authentic self, reflecting who you are at your core.

- Encourages a life that is congruent with your true identity and beliefs.

G. **Clarity of Purpose:**
- Offers a clear and concise statement that encapsulates the essence of your mission.
- Serves as a brief reminder of your life's purpose and direction.

H. **Flexibility and Adaptability:**
- Acknowledges that life is dynamic and subject to change.
- Allows for flexibility and adaptation while maintaining core principles.

2. **Living in Alignment:** Review and consider your mission statement often. Verify that the choices and actions you make align with the principles outlined in your resolution. By embracing your goal as your own, you create a deep sense of purpose and fulfillment. Regularly reviewing and considering your mission statement, then can develop into a meditative and peaceful routine. It acts as a compass, ensuring that all of your decisions and actions are in perfect harmony with the tenets of your goal. Accepting your mission proposes making the conscious choice to give meaning and fulfillment to every aspect of your life.

A well-rounded mission statement weaves these elements into a cohesive narrative, creating a powerful framework that provides clarity and focus and resonates with your authentic self. The mission statement is like a rock in the midst of life's chaos, reminding you of your purpose and calling you to live true to who you are. It turns the intangible concepts of values and interests into a concrete road plan that leads you to a life that is authentically you.

**Embracing Growth and Change** - Embracing growth and change is a mindset that welcomes the transformative power of evolving experiences, fostering adaptability, and enabling personal development. Accepting this action opens doors to new perspectives and opportunities, allowing you to navigate life's uncertainties with resilience and courage, ultimately leading to a more enriched and fulfilling journey.

1. **The Dynamic Nature of Life:** In its most basic form, life is a dynamic journey marked by an ongoing stream of encounters, difficulties, and personal development. Embracing this journey involves recognizing that change is inevitable and a powerful catalyst for personal development. Each twist and turn, every peak and valley, presents an opportunity for learning, adaptation, and evolution. A crucial mindset in navigating life's spectrum is the willingness to evolve. This commitment

goes beyond merely accepting change; it entails actively seeking opportunities for growth and transformation. Just as a spectrum encompasses a wide range of colors, the voyage offers diverse experiences that contribute to the richness of your personal narrative.

**Learning from Change:** Difficulties are an essential part of being human. When you see obstacles as chances to improve your adaptability and progress, you develop resilience in the face of adversity enhancing your life's richness and insight. Although they are sometimes viewed as barriers, challenges are essential parts of this exciting adventure and they serve as stepping stones for development and knowledge rather than as stumbling blocks. Reframing adversities as learning opportunities allows you to see them in a different light. The lessons you acquire from overcoming obstacles not only help you grow personally but also add depth and wisdom to your life.

In essence, navigating life's dynamic spectrum involves:

- A continuous dance with change.
- An openness to the lessons it brings.
- A commitment to evolving into the best version of yourself.

This active participation in the ebb and flow of existence guarantees that every stage adds to the colorful tapestry of your experiences, development, and learning that make up your individual path. To embrace the fluidity of life is to intentionally engage in its dynamic fabric and allow a variety of events to come together to create a vibrant and evolving story that shapes your own road to personal development.

**Mindful Decision-Making** - Making decisions with mindfulness entails deliberate awareness as well as taking the present, values, and outcomes into account. It fosters choices that are in line with your sincerity and intention. Mindful decisions gives you the ability to deal with the challenges of life in a clear and honest manner, helping you to develop a closer relationship with your inner self and point you in the direction of real fulfillment and significant influence.

1. **Conscious Choices:** Each choice you make adds to the overall picture of your existence. Making thoughtful decisions involves weighing options in relation to your mission, values, and long-term objectives. Rendering deliberate decisions is like using paintbrushes to color your life; every brushstroke adds to your rich tapestry. Mindful decision-making involves considering the immediate consequences of your actions and evaluating their alignment with your broader aspirations and values. By taking a moment to pause and reflect on the implications of your

choices, you empower yourself to steer in directions that resonate deeply with your authentic self.

2. **Balancing Short-Term and Long-Term Goals:** While addressing immediate needs and desires is essential, consider the long-term impact of your choices. Balancing short-term gratification with long-term vision is akin to orchestrating a symphony where each note contributes to the harmonious melody of your life. Maintaining a strategic focus on long-term goals ensures that your decisions are reactive and proactive in shaping your desired future. This delicate balance fosters a sense of fulfillment and purpose as you navigate the ever-evolving landscape with intentionality and foresight. Ultimately, you craft a life imbued with depth, meaning, and fulfillment by embracing conscious choices and pairing short-term pleasures with long-term aspirations.

In this delicate dance, the artistry lies not just in the decisions themselves but in the synchronicity created by their alignment with your broader life vision. The interplay between short-term satisfaction and a strategic focus on long-term goals ensures that your life's canvas is rich in diversity and possesses a coherence that enhances its overall beauty. Through these deliberate choices, informed by a balance of immediacy and foresight, you can craft a well-rounded and fulfilling masterpiece that reflects the essence of who you are and/or aspire to be.

**Building a Supportive Environment** - Building a supportive environment involves fostering spaces, relationships, and practices that encourage personal growth, well-being, and a sense of belonging. It entails nurturing an ecosystem where you feel empowered to thrive, surrounded by empathy, encouragement, and resources that nourish your journey towards fulfillment and connection.

1. **Surrounding Yourself with Positivity:** Examine your living spaces on a physical and mental level. Being in a positive environment makes it easier for you to deal with the ups and downs of life with resilience and joy. Your home can become a haven for your wellbeing when it is designed harmoniously and filled with features that are uplifting and motivating. Positive physical surroundings, such as the warmth of natural light, the brilliance of colors, or the significant objects around you, provide the groundwork for a buoyant mindset as you negotiate the twists and turns of existence.

2. **Developing Supportive Relationships:** Having deep relationships with other people is essential to living a happy life. Develop connections with others who uphold your values and enhance your wellbeing. In trying circumstances, a network of support can offer strength and encouragement. By actively seeking out and cultivating relationships that are consistent with your beliefs, you create

a support system that serves as a bulwark during difficult times. These relationships grow into pillars of support, resiliency, and joyous laughter, providing a safe space to express the range of colors in your life.

In essence, the act of surrounding yourself with positivity, both in your physical spaces and relational landscapes, is an intentional brushstroke on the canvas of your life. It transforms the mundane into the extraordinary and infuses your journey with a vibrant energy that propels you forward with resilience, purpose, and a profound sense of joy.

**Holistic Well-Being** - Holistic well-being encompasses nurturing physical, mental, emotional, and spiritual dimensions, fostering a balanced and harmonious life. It extends beyond mere physical health, encompassing the cultivation of resilience, self-awareness, and a deep sense of purpose, ultimately leading to a life rich in fulfillment and authenticity.

1. **Mind, Body, and Soul:** Acknowledge the interconnected nature of your mind, body, and soul. Prioritize activities which contribute to holistic well-being, encompassing mental, emotional, physical, and spiritual dimensions. Understanding the interconnected nature of your mind, body, and soul is like recognizing the synergy of a well-choreographed dance. Each element influences

the others, and prioritizing activities contributing to holistic well-being becomes a conscious commitment to maintaining this harmonious twirl.

2. **Self-Care as a Priority:** Make self-care as a firm facet of your daily routine. In a world often filled with hustle and bustle, making self-care a non-negotiable aspect of your everyday practice is a radical act of self-compassion. It's more than just a luxury; it's a fundamental necessity for navigating life's spectrum with strength and resilience. Self-care isn't a one-size-fits-all concept; it's a tailored practice that reflects your unique needs and preferences. Whether engaging in regular exercise that invigorates your body, practicing mindfulness techniques that soothe your mind, or indulging in leisure activities that bring joy to your soul, self-care is a multifaceted approach for nurturing every aspect of your being. By embracing self-care as a priority, you are investing in your immediate well-being and fostering the long-term resilience needed to navigate life's twists and turns. It's an ongoing commitment to yourself, ensuring that amidst life's demands, you remain grounded, balanced, and equipped to face whatever comes your way with grace and vitality.

**The Pursuit of Meaning** - The pursuit of meaning involves aligning actions with values, fostering connections, and contributing to a purpose larger than yourself, creating a fulfilling and purpose-driven life. By actively seeking meaning, you are invited to set out on a deep path of self-discovery, where you may find joy in serving a cause bigger than yourself and develop meaningful connections with others.

1. **Meaningful Experiences:** Infuse meaning into your life by engaging in experiences that resonate with your values and passions. Seek activities that contribute to a sense of purpose and fulfillment, adding depth to your life's spectrum. In the vast canvas of life, meaningful experiences act as vibrant brushstrokes that add richness and depth to the overall composition. Infusing your life with activities that resonate with your beliefs and desires creates a tapestry woven with threads of purpose and fulfillment. It's about seeking moments and engagements that align with the authentic essence of who you are. These experiences become the colorful tones that paint your life's spectrum in hues of joy and satisfaction.

2. **Contributing to Others:** The act of giving back and contributing to the well-being of others impacts significantly to a meaningful life. Embracing compassion towards others is like sharing the palette of your profound experiences. Giving back, whether through small acts of kindness, dedicated volunteering, or meaningful

mentorship, transcends individual lives and creates a beautiful interplay of colors in the shared human experience. Your contributions become interconnected threads, weaving a narrative of compassion, empathy, and collective growth. It's a reciprocal dance where the more you contribute, the more profound your sense of purpose becomes. This intertwining of meaningful experiences and contributions to others creates a symphony of purpose that resonates through the spectrum of your life, leaving an indelible mark on the canvas of your connections.

**Balancing Ambition and Contentment** - Balancing ambition and contentment requires setting ambitious goals while appreciating and finding satisfaction in the present, fostering both growth and gratitude. It involves striving for aspirations while cherishing the blessings of the present, nurturing a mindset that celebrates progress while embracing the beauty of the journey.

1. **Ambition as a Driving Force:** Embrace ambition as a driving force, motivating you to pursue your passions and make a positive impact. Ambition adds vibrancy to your life's spectrum. It serves as a dynamic force propelling you forward on the path toward your goals and aspirations, infusing your life's spectrum with energy and purpose. It's the flame that ignites passion, fuels resilience,

and motivates you to impact the world positively. Embracing ambition means acknowledging your potential and having the courage to dream big, pushing the boundaries of what you thought possible.

2. **Savoring Contentment:** While ambition is crucial to success and fulfillment, savoring contentment in the present moment is equally important. Appreciate the journey, celebrate achievements, and find joy in the simplicity of everyday experiences. However, amid pursuing ambitious goals, pausing and cherishing happiness in the existing point in time is essential. Simultaneously, ambition drives you toward future achievements, and contentment anchors you in the richness of the current experience. It involves appreciating the journey, celebrating the small victories, and finding joy in the uncomplicatedness of ordinary moments.

Balancing ambition with contentment creates a composed life continuum where a deep appreciation for the beauty of the present complements the pursuit of goals. In this delicate equilibrium, ambition becomes a force that propels you forward, while contentment acts as the grounding and stabilizing factor. It's the art of appreciating the progress you've made, relishing the beauty of the journey, and finding fulfillment in reaching the destination and the steps taken along the way. This balance creates a life spectrum that is not only vibrant with ambition but also harmonious with the tranquility of contentment.

## Reflection and Adaptation

1. **Regular Life Audits:** Periodically conduct life audits to assess your current alignment with values, goals, and mission. Reflection allows for adaptation, ensuring that your life's spectrum evolves in resonance with your authentic self. This process serves as a powerful tool for self-reflection and self-awareness. By periodically assessing your alignment with values, goals, and mission, you create a space for intentional reflection. This reflection enables you to recognize areas needing adjustment, ensuring your life resonates with your evolving genuine identity. Life is dynamic, and conducting these audits allows you to adapt and realign as needed, fostering a continuous and conscious journey of personal growth.

2. **Flexibility in Goals:** Be flexible in your goals and expectations. Embracing flexibility allows you to adjust your course while staying true to your core values. Flexibility in goal-setting is a crucial element of navigating life's variety of experiences effectively. While setting ambitious targets provides direction and motivation, adopting the plasticity to change acknowledges this unpredictability, requiring adjustments to your path as unexpected

opportunities or challenges may arise. Being flexible in your goals means staying within your values and continuing your mission. It's about maintaining a balance between a clear direction and the adaptability needed to navigate unforeseen twists in the journey. This dynamic approach ensures that you remain resilient, responsive, and true to your core values as you navigate life's ever-changing landscape.

**Living a Legacy** - Living a legacy is about weaving a tapestry of influence through every interaction and decision, inspiring future generations with a narrative of purpose, compassion, and meaningful engagement with the world. It involves consciously shaping your actions, values, and contributions, leaving a positive and lasting impact.

1. **Defining Your Legacy:** Consider the legacy you want to leave behind. What impact do you aspire to have on others and the world? Defining your legacy involves introspection and reflection on the profound influence you wish to make. It's about considering the values and principles that guide your life and the narrative you want to leave behind. Your "why" becomes the anchor that adds a profound sense of purpose and continuity to your journey through life's spectrum. This deliberate self-awareness shapes the trajectory of

your actions, aligning them with the legacy you aim to create.

2. **Intentional Contributions:** To live intentionally involves making choices that contribute positively to fulfill your "why." Whether through personal relationships, professional endeavors, or community involvement, your intentional contributions shape the narrative of your impact. Living with intentional contributions is a dynamic and ongoing commitment to making choices that align with your defined legacy. It's a conscious effort to influence your surroundings positively, be it through nurturing personal connections, excelling in your professional pursuits, or actively participating in social initiatives. Each intentional contribution is a brushstroke on the canvas of your legacy, contributing to the larger narrative of your impact on the world. By approaching life with intentionality, you craft a meaningful and purpose-driven journey that resonates with your core values and leaves a lasting imprint on the lives of others.

### A Life Well-Lived

As you stand at the intersection of your past, present, and future, may you recognize the masterpiece that is your life's spectrum. "Living Your Spectrum" encompasses the essence of intentional living – a dynamic, purposeful, and meaningful existence. It's about weaving together moments of growth, connection, and fulfillment as you navigate the canvas of existence with authenticity and purpose.

In this canvas of your life, you are both the artist and the subject. With each brushstroke, you contribute to the unfolding tapestry of your experiences, connections, and personal growth. May your journey through the spectrum of life be a reflection of your authentic self, guided by your values, fueled by passion, and rich with the joy of a life well-lived.

# CHAPTER 11

# "A Call to Action: Empowering Change Through Purposeful Engagement"

## Answering the Call to Action for a Better Tomorrow:

Now that you have garnered the necessary skills to grow and change with grace and vitality, it is expected that you will ponder your role in shaping a better tomorrow in a world filled with complexities, challenges, and opportunities. Whether advocating for social justice, combating climate change, or promoting education, a call to action mobilizes you toward a meaningful change. Here we explore the concept of a call to action, its significance, and how it empowers you to become an agent of positive transformation in your community and beyond.

In answering the call to action for a better tomorrow, you are driven by a sense of responsibility and a desire to make a difference. The understanding that personal change starts with each individual is at the heart of this motivation. You can take a major initiative in areas that align with your values and passions if you recognize the potential effect you can have.

The interdependence of global challenges and the significance of addressing them holistically are emphasized in this chapter. There is seldom a problem in a vacuum, and finding solutions frequently calls for collaboration across boundaries, industries, and communities. Fostering a collaborative and team-oriented atmosphere can help you exert more influence and accelerate systemic change on a larger scale.

It provides the inspiration and guidance to answer the call through engaging narratives, real-world examples, and practical strategies. It inspires you to push the boundaries of your comfort zone, question the status quo, and support causes that are authentically meaningful to you. You may be a force for good in the world, fostering a more fair, just, and sustainable future by putting your passion, abilities, and resources to use.

## Understanding the Call to Action:

A call to action is a compelling invitation or directive that urges you to take specific steps or initiatives towards a desired goal or outcome. It serves as a rallying cry, motivating you to mobilize your efforts, resources, and talents towards a desired purpose or cause. Whether it's a grassroots movement, a social media campaign, or a global initiative, a call to action galvanizes you to rise up and make a difference in the world around you.

A call to action transcends mere encouragement; it embodies a sense of urgency and importance that compels you to act decisively. It serves as a catalyst for change, igniting the passion and purpose within you and your community alike. It is a plea that can resonate deeply with your values and beliefs, prompting you to align your actions with your convictions.

Furthermore, a call to action is not limited by scale or scope; it can manifest in various forms, from local grassroots initiatives to global campaigns. Whether it's a community cleanup effort, a petition for policy reform, or a viral social media challenge, each call to action has the power to spark transformation and inspire collective action. By leveraging the power of technology and social networks, you can amplify your voice and reach a broader audience, mobilize support, and drive change on a larger dimension.

A call to action also increases your sense of empowerment by serving as a reminder of your ability to influence real change.

It motivates you to push the envelope, oppose the current quo, and support causes that align with your beliefs. By doing this, you take an active role in influencing the environment, advancing society, and building a better future.

## Significance of a Call to Action:

A call to action's transformative potential to uplift people and spur collective action toward significant change accounts for its relevance. A call to action is more than just words of encouragement; it is a symbol of empowerment that serves as a constant reminder to people of their innate ability to affect change and improve the world and encourages them to accept responsibility for their part in influencing the future by instilling a sense of agency.

Moreover, a call to action gives individuals a clear direction and purpose, guiding their efforts toward constructive and impactful endeavors. Outlining specific steps or initiatives helps you channel your energy and passion toward tangible goals and outcomes. This clarity of purpose fuels motivation and fosters a sense of focus and determination, enabling you to overcome obstacles and stay committed to your cause.

In addition, a call to action is essential for bridging the awareness and action gaps. Increasing public awareness of important issues is frequently the first step in bringing about change in today's linked world with easy access to information. But awareness on its own is insufficient; it needs to be supported by proactive and practical measures. A call to action inspires you to turn this awareness into meaningful action, turning you from a bystander to an engaged contributor to the pursuit of justice and progress.

A call to action also acts as a stimulus for group mobilization and cooperation. Through uniting people around a similar goal or cause, one can transcend individual differences and mobilize collective strength, fostering a sense of solidarity and unity. A call to action is a strategy that can be used by grassroots movements, social media campaigns, or international organizations to mobilize people to take action and change the world for the better.

A call to action is important because it may empower you, give you a clear sense of purpose, close the awareness gap, and inspire group members to work together toward significant change. As an agent of change, you can help create a more equal, just, and brighter future for everyone by accepting your position and responding to the call to action.

### Components of an Effective Call to Action:
1. **Clarity of Purpose:** A compelling call to action begins with a clear and concise articulation of the desired goal or outcome. It defines the problem or issue at hand, identifies the stakeholders involved, and outlines the specific actions or initiatives required to address it.

2. **Sense of Urgency:** To ignite change, a call to action often conveys a sense of urgency or importance. It emphasizes the immediate need for intervention or shift, highlighting the consequences of inaction and inspiring a sense of responsibility and commitment among individuals.

3. **Accessibility and Inclusivity:** An effective call to action is accessible and inclusive, welcoming individuals from diverse backgrounds, perspectives, and experiences to participate. It removes barriers to engagement, fosters a culture of belonging and inclusivity, and ensures that everyone has a voice and a role to play in the collective effort.

4. **Mobilization and Engagement:** A successful call to action mobilizes individuals to actively engage in the cause or initiative. It leverages various channels and platforms to reach and inspire a broad audience, encourage meaningful participation and collaboration, and foster a sense of community and solidarity among supporters.

5. **Measurable Impact:** An impactful call to action is grounded in measurable outcomes and influence. It sets clear targets, benchmarks, and indicators to track progress and evaluate success, enabling stakeholders to assess the effectiveness of their efforts and adapt strategies accordingly.

## Examples of Effective Calls to Action:

1. **Environmental Conservation:** A call to action to combat climate change may include initiatives such as reducing carbon emissions, promoting renewable energy sources, and advocating for sustainable practices in industries and communities worldwide. It mobilizes individuals, governments, and businesses to take concrete steps towards mitigating the effects of climate change and preserving the planet for future generations.

2. **Social Justice:** A call to action for social justice may involve addressing systemic inequalities and injustices, advocating for the rights of marginalized communities, and promoting policies and initiatives that promote equality and inclusion. It rallies activists, advocates, and allies to stand up against discrimination, oppression, and injustice in all its forms.

3. **Public Health:** In response to global health crises such as a pandemic, a call to action may involve promoting vaccination, adhering to public health guidelines, and supporting healthcare workers on the frontlines. It mobilizes individuals and communities to prioritize public health measures and work together to prevent the spread of infectious diseases and safeguard public well-being.

## Empowering You to Answer the Call:

1. **Education and Awareness:** Empowering individuals to answer the call to action begins with education and awareness. By raising awareness about pressing issues, providing access to accurate information and resources, and fostering dialogue and discussion, you can become more informed and an engaged advocate for change.

2. **Building Coalitions and Partnerships:** Collaboration and partnership are essential for amplifying the impact of a call to action. By building coalitions, alliances, and partnerships with like-minded organizations, communities, and stakeholders, you can leverage a collective strength and resources to advance your goals and initiatives.

3. **Grassroots Organizing:** Grassroots organizing plays a crucial role in mobilizing individuals and communities to take action. By organizing grassroots campaigns, rallies, protests, and events, you can raise awareness, build momentum, and effect change at the local, national, and global levels on behalf of your meaningful causes.

4. **Advocacy and Activism:** Advocacy and activism are powerful tools for driving social and political change. By advocating for policy reform, mobilizing public support, and holding decision-makers accountable, you can influence change and advance the causes you believe in.

A call to action acts as a beacon of hope and possibility, empowering you to transform your aspirations into tangible actions and outcomes. Whether it's advocating for social justice, protecting the environment, or promoting public health, a call to action inspires you to stand up, speak out, and make a difference in the world around you. By answering the call, you can harness your power and create a brighter, more equitable, and sustainable future for generations to come.

# CONCLUSION

## "Embracing Your Rainbow Journey"

As we reach the culmination of our exploration into personal fulfillment, the pages of this book reflect a journey toward understanding, resilience, and the vibrant tapestry of a life well-lived. "Finding Your Rainbow in a Sky Full of Clouds" encapsulates the essence of this odyssey, emphasizing the beauty that emerges from navigating life's challenges with courage and intentionality.

### A Recap of Key Strategies and Insights

Our journey began with an overview of the quest for personal fulfillment. A journey is unique to each individual yet bound by shared human experiences. Through chapters like "Embracing the Storm," "Crafting Your Palette," and "Connecting with Others," we delved into strategies and insights designed to empower you in your pursuit of a meaningful and fulfilling life.

As we reach the culmination of our journey, let's take a moment to reflect on the key strategies and insights that have been uncovered. You have equipped yourself with powerful tools, from recognizing the clouds in life to setting meaningful goals, from cultivating emotional intelligence to navigating challenges with resilience. Maintaining a positive mindset, fostering empathy in your interactions, and building a robust support network are crucial components of your transformative expedition. Each chapter has contributed to the foundation of knowledge and skills needed to discover your rainbow in a sky full of clouds.

### Navigating Life's Storms

Life is, inevitably, a series of storms and clear skies. The storms represent challenges, setbacks, and adversities that test your resilience and shape your character. As we discussed in "Embracing the Storm," the key is not to avoid these squalls but to face them with courage, understanding that they are integral to the narrative of personal growth.

Embracing life's storms means recognizing that challenges and adversities are inherent to personal growth. Facing them with courage builds resilience, shaping a narrative of strength, wisdom, and continuous self-discovery. It's through navigating storms that you uncover your true capabilities and resilience, allowing you to emerge stronger and more resilient on the other side.

## Crafting Your Palette: Setting Goals and Dreams

Crafting personal goals and dreams is an art, like selecting vibrant colors for your life's masterpiece. Aligned with values and passions, these goals become the brushstrokes defining your unique journey. Just as an artist meticulously chooses hues, thoughtful goal-setting creates a roadmap that leads you through the diverse landscapes of your rainbow existence, painting a rich and fulfilling life.

Setting personal goals and dreams, as explored in "Crafting Your Palette," is akin to selecting the colors defining your stunning success. Through thoughtful goal-setting aligned with your values and passions, you create a roadmap that guides you through the varied landscapes of your rainbow journey.

## Building Resilience in Turbulent Times

In "Weathering the Changes," we explored the art of building resilience. This skill allows you not only to withstand the turbulence of life but also to emerge stronger and more adaptable. Resilience is the compass that keeps you on course when the winds of change blow and empowers you to navigate life's spectrum with grace.

Building resilience is more than weathering life's storms; it's about harnessing inner strength to thrive amidst adversity. Like a sturdy vessel navigating rough seas, resilience empowers you to navigate life's spectrum with courage, adaptability, and grace, ensuring you emerge from challenges stronger and more resilient than before.

## Shifting Perspective for Positivity

"Rainbow Mindset" delved into the transformative power of perspective. By developing and nurturing a positive mindset, you infuse each color of your life's spectrum with brightness. This shift in perspective is not about denying challenges but about embracing the potential for growth and joy, even in the face of adversity.

Embracing a rainbow mindset entails acknowledging life's challenges while choosing to focus on opportunities and growth. By shifting your perspective, you invite joy and resilience into every aspect of your journey, transforming obstacles into stepping stones toward a brighter, more fulfilling life.

## Unveiling Your Potential

"Unveiling Your Potential" was an invitation to explore the richness within yourself – the unique strengths and talents that define your authenticity. This chapter encouraged you to embark on a lifelong journey of self-discovery, understanding that your potential is boundless and continually evolving.

Embarking on the journey of self-discovery is not merely about uncovering hidden talents but also about embracing the process of growth and evolution. By recognizing that our potential knows no bounds, we empower ourselves to continually explore, learn, and evolve, shaping a more authentic and fulfilling life journey.

## Finding Joy in the Midst of Adversity

"Dancing in the Rain" explored the profound art of finding joy even in the midst of life's storms. Like a melody, joy can be woven into your existence's rhythm. It's a testament to your resilience and a celebration of the human spirit's ability to find light in the darkest times.

Finding joy amidst life's storms is not about denying pain or challenges but about embracing the inherent resilience within you. It's a conscious choice to seek beauty and positivity, transforming adversity into opportunities for growth and creating a harmonious melody of life's experiences.

## Connecting with Others: Building Supportive Relationships

In "Connecting with Others," we delved into the importance of relationships—the threads that weave the fabric of a fulfilling life. Meaningful connections with family, friends, and colleagues provide support, understanding, and shared moments that enrich the spectrum of your journey.

Connections with others form the rich tapestry of life, offering shared experiences, support, and understanding. These relationships are the threads that strengthen the fabric of your journey, adding depth, color, and warmth to the canvas of our existence. They provide a sense of belonging, mutual growth, and the joy of shared moments that contribute to the vibrancy of life's spectrum.

## Living Yor Spectrum: Creating a Fulfilling and Meaningful Life

Finally, in "Living Your Spectrum," we explored the concept of intentional living. By understanding your values, passions, and the dynamic nature of life, you are empowered to create a fulfilling and meaningful life that reflects the unique hues of your spectrum.

Living your spectrum is the art of intentional living, a conscious weaving of your values, passions, and an appreciation for life's dynamic nature. Empowered by this understanding, you craft a life that resonates with authenticity and meaning, each moment a brushstroke adding vibrant hues to your unique canvas. It's a continual process of self-discovery, growth, and purposeful navigation through the ever-evolving landscape of your existence.

## ▪ Embracing the Masterpiece of Your Life

As you stand at the conclusion of this book, envision your life as a masterpiece—a canvas painted with the colors of your experiences, relationships, and personal growth. Each chapter is a stroke, and each principle is a hue contributing to the tapestry of your existence.

As you reflect on the pages turned and principles embraced, see your life as a masterpiece. Each chapter, a brushstroke, blending experiences, relationships, and growth into a canvas that tells the story of your journey. The beauty lies in the harmonious interplay of colors—a symphony of moments that form the unique masterpiece that is your life. Embrace the canvas, for it is a living artwork in perpetual creation, shaped by your choices, resilience, and the ever-changing palette of life.

## ▪ Intentional Living

This book is not just a collection of words; it's an invitation to embark on a journey of self-discovery, resilience, and intentional living. The principles shared here are tools in your toolkit, ready to accompany you as you navigate the ever-changing landscape of your life.

Consider these principles as trusted companions, residing in your toolkit. Armed with wisdom, you navigate life's dynamic terrain, forging a path that aligns with your true self. May the journey unfold with exploration, growth, and the unwavering belief in the beauty of your unique story.

## A Call to Action

A call to action is an effective instruction that persuades people to do particular actions toward a desired result. It enables you to see your potential for change and motivates you to actively participate in creating a better future.

A call to action closes the awareness gap and turns inactive observers into active participants in pursuing development and progress by articulating a clear purpose and inspiring a group effort. It inspires you to take action and improve your community by fostering solidarity, hope, and significant change, whether fighting for social justice, advancing education, or opposing climate change.

## The Rainbow Journey Continues

Remember, your rainbow journey is ongoing. Life's spectrum unfolds with each passing moment, offering new challenges, opportunities, and moments of joy. Embrace the ebb and flow, the storms and clear skies, and dance within the rhythm of your unique existence.

Your rainbow journey is an ever-evolving symphony, a continuous dance with life's spectrum. In each moment, embrace the unfolding tapestry of challenges, opportunities, and joys. Navigate the ebb and flow with resilience, savoring the storms and clear skies alike. Dance to the rhythm of your unique existence, for the beauty lies not just in the hues but in the graceful movement through the kaleidoscope of experiences that shape your ongoing masterpiece. Embrace the journey, for it is the process that unveils the vibrant colors of your evolving life.

### Your Story, Your Rainbow

In the vast sky of human experience, your story is a unique constellation—a rainbow waiting to be discovered. The clouds may cast shadows, but it's within those shadows that the brilliance of your colors becomes most vivid. As you continue your journey, may you find the strength to weather the storms, the wisdom to savor the sunshine, and the joy to dance in the rain.

Your life's narrative, akin to a celestial spectacle, unfolds with its own luminous hues and intricate patterns. Amidst life's trials and triumphs, your resilience shines brightest, painting the sky with the vibrant colors of your spirit. Embrace the storms and cherish the sunshine, for within each lies the essence of your iridescent journey.

### A Gratitude for the Journey

Thank you for allowing this book to be a companion on your rainbow journey. It's been an honor to explore these principles with you, and I encourage you to carry the wisdom gained forward. May your life be a testament to the beauty that emerges when you navigate with resilience, pursue fulfillment with intentionality, and create a spectrum that reflects your true essence.

As we part ways, remember that your journey is an ever-evolving masterpiece. Carry the principles within, let resilience guide you, and paint your spectrum authentically. May your days be a testament to the transformative power of intentional living, reflecting the radiant beauty of your unique essence.

## Here's to Your Rainbow Journey

As you turn the last page, remember that your rainbow journey is ongoing. May you continue to embrace the storms, savor the clear skies, and dance through the entire spectrum of your existence. Here's to a well-lived life that radiates with the vibrancy of your unique colors.

As you close this chapter, let it be a reminder that your life is an ever-unfolding story. Embrace the ongoing journey, finding joy in every hue. May you navigate challenges with resilience, bask in moments of clarity, and dance through the entire spectrum, creating a life that resonates with your authentic colors.

## ■ Encouragement for Your Personal Journey

Embarking on the rainbow journey requires understanding the clouds that may cast shadows and an unwavering belief in the potential for radiant hues to emerge. The principles explored—from resilience and positivity to connecting with others and embracing your spectrum – form a roadmap, guiding you through the diverse landscapes of your life.

Embarking on the journey toward personal fulfillment is a choice and a commitment to self-discovery, growth, and resilience. As you stand at the precipice of change, remember that the clouds in your life are not obstacles but opportunities for transformation. Embrace the challenges, for within them lies the potential to uncover the vibrant hues of your unique rainbow. Your journey is an ongoing process, a dynamic tapestry of experiences that shape and redefine your path.

Take with you the knowledge that resilience is not just a response to adversity but a state of being, a mindset that propels you forward even when the clouds gather. You have the wisdom to navigate challenges, the strength to maintain a positive mindset, and the compassion to connect with others on their journeys. Your support network is your anchor, grounding you in times of turbulence and celebrating your victories.

In closing, remember that personal fulfillment is not a destination but a continuous journey. As you step forward, embrace the unknown with courage and optimism. Your rainbow awaits, painting the sky with the hues of your unique strengths, experiences, and dreams. May your journey be filled with resilience, positivity, and the unwavering belief that, amidst the clouds, your rainbow shines brightest. Go forth with purpose and the brilliance that only you can bring!

# Reference

Digital Mindset: Thriving in the Age of Data, Algorithms, and AI. https://www.revidd.com/blogs/mastering-a-digital-mindset-in-the-era-of-algorithms-and-machine-learning.

Diving Into The Core Competencies of SEL: Self-Management. https://www.tlpnyc.com/blog/diving-into-the-core-competencies-of-sel-self-management.

Mindsets for Success: Essential Strategies to Elevate Your Game. https://seriosity.com/minsets-for-success/

Cultivating a Growth Mindset: A Comprehensive Guide for Unlocking Potential and Fostering Lifelong Learning - eduKate Tuition Centre. https://edukatesingapore.com/2023/04/06/cultivating-a-growth-mindset-a-comprehensive-guide-for-unlocking-potential-and-fostering-lifelong-learning/

Empowered Healing: How To Integrate Science & Intuition. https://www.wholistic.com/blog/empowered-healing-how-to-integrate-science-intuition

15 Inspiring Personal Growth Journal Prompts for Self-Reflection - Luciepo. https://luciepo.com/personal-growth-journal-prompts/

10 Daily Habits That Will Change Your Life | Week Plan. https://weekplan.net/Daily-Habits-That-Will-Change-Your-Life/

Your Best Year Ever -A Journey of Introspection! - Living Healthy List. https://livinghealthylist.com/personal-development/your-best-year-ever-a-journey-of-introspection/

Smart Goals: 5 Credible Ways To Achieve Your Dream. https://makealivingwriting.com/smart-goals-achieve-your-dream/

Unlock Your Full Potential: Strategies for Personal Growth | GEYN. http://www.geteverythingyouneed.com/strategies-for-personal-growth/

10 Morning Habits That Will change your life. https://www.baltistantoday.com/2023/08/10-morning-habits-that-will-change-your.html

How to Build Rock-Solid Self-Esteem. https://spencerinstitute.com/how-to-build-rock-solid-self-esteem/

Developing a Personal Development Plan with Your Life Coach. https://lifecoachtraining.co/category/personal-development/developing-a-personal-development-plan-with-your-life-coach/

The Strength of Resilience • 1 Love Poems. https://1lovepoems.com/miscellaneous/poems-about-resilience/

Battling Burnout: Finding Balance in a Hectic World - Develefy Consulting. https://develefy.com/blog/battling-burnout-finding-balance-in-a-hectic-world/

Making Healthy Choices While Grieving. https://oceancountycremationservice.com/blogs/blog-entries/1/Our-Blogs-Ocean-County-Cremation-Service/164/Making-Healthy-Choices-While-Grieving.html

The Power of Passion and Perseverance. https://www.dorosstech.com/2023/03/Power-Passion.html

Surrender to What-Is | Thoth Readings. https://thothreadings.com/surrender-to-what-is/

Unlocking Personal Growth: The Power of Self-Discovery Worksheets - Quenza. https://quenza.com/blog/knowledge-base/self-discovery-worksheets/

Importance of Mental Health - military parenting. https://militaryparenting.org/importance-of-mental-health/

Cultivating a Positive Mindset for Personal Growth | Success Way. https://success-way.net/cultivating-a-positive-mindset-for-personal-growth/

The ADHD Negativity Bias. https://www.adhdconfident.com/post/the-adhd-negativity-bias

18 Practical Ways to Show Up for Yourself in Life. https://lauraconteuse.com/show-up-for-yourself/

GRASPED The Power of Relationships and Communication - GRASPED Digital. https://grasped.

digital/chatgpt/grasped-the-power-of-relationships-and-communication/

5 Pillars Of Health Teachers Can Use To Feel Their Best Right Now. https://www.forbes.com/sites/robynshulman/2020/03/29/5-pillars-of-health-teachers-can-use-to-feel-their-best-right-now/

What do therapists have to say about Self Care?. https://www.xeniacounseling.org/post/what-do-therapists-have-to-say-about-self-care

Amazonite - Chakra Balancing and Healing – The Honey Pot Energy and Art. https://energyandarts.com/products/amazonite

# About the Author

Teresa B. Graves, LPC-S is a Licensed Professional Counselor with more than 30 years of experience in the field of mental health. She has assisted her clients with navigating the most turbulent moments of their lives and had the pleasure of witnessing much of the growth, change, and personal development described within the pages of this book. She currently lives in Cypress, Texas with her husband and two dogs.

Made in the USA
Columbia, SC
25 May 2024

f3c5f76d-fb30-4c71-9d0e-cb194fcccc0eR01